500 KNIVES

500 KNIVES

CELEBRATING TRADITIONAL AND INNOVATIVE DESIGNS

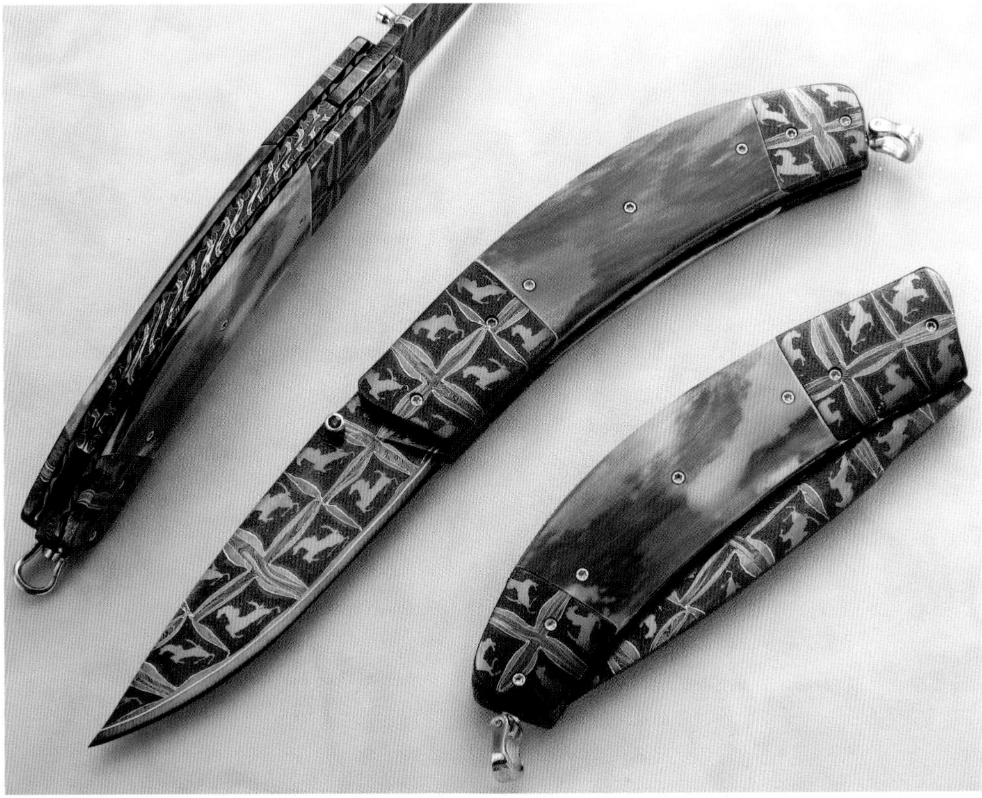

A Division of Sterling Publishing Co., Inc.
New York / London

SENIOR EDITOR
Marthe Le Van

EDITOR
Julie Hale

ART DIRECTOR
Kay Holmes Stafford

COVER DESIGNER
Celia Naranjo

FRONT COVER
John L. Jensen
Nuibiru, 2008

BACK COVER, FROM TOP LEFT
Dusty Moulton
Raptor, 2004

Johan Gustafsson
Symphony, 2005

Owen Wood
Art Nouveau Folding Knife, 2008

Ronald Best
Untitled, 2008

SPINE
Peter Mason
Phantom Dagger, 2007

FRONT FLAP, FROM TOP
Buddy Weston
Life II, 2004

Dennis E. Friedly
Gent's Blue Bowie, 2007

BACK FLAP, FROM TOP
David Broadwell
Persian, 2000

R.J. Martin
Dress Havoc Flipper, 2004

PAGE 3
Johan Gustafsson
Mosaic Fighter, 2003

PAGE 5
Shosui Takeda
Ken-Nata Hunter, 2007

Library of Congress Cataloging-in-Publication Data

500 knives : celebrating traditional & innovative designs / senior editor, Marthe Le Van. — 1st ed.
p. cm.
Includes index.
ISBN 978-1-57990-873-7 (pb-pbk. with deluxe flaps : alk. paper)
1. Knives. 2. Knifesmiths. 3. Decoration and ornament. I. Le Van, Marthe. II. Title: Five hundred knives.
TS380.A16 2009
621.9'32—dc22
2008049562

10 9 8 7 6 5 4 3 2 1

First Edition

Published by Lark Books, A Division of
Sterling Publishing Co., Inc.
387 Park Avenue South, New York, NY 10016

Distributed in Canada by Sterling Publishing,
c/o Canadian Manda Group, 165 Dufferin Street
Toronto, Ontario, Canada M6K 3H6

Distributed in the United Kingdom by GMC Distribution Services,
Castle Place, 166 High Street, Lewes, East Sussex, England BN7 1XU

Distributed in Australia by Capricorn Link (Australia) Pty Ltd.,
P.O. Box 704, Windsor, NSW 2756 Australia

If you have questions or comments about this book, please contact:
Lark Books
67 Broadway
Asheville, NC 28801
828-253-0467

Manufactured in China

ISBN 13: 978-1-57990-873-7

For information about custom editions, special sales, premium and corporate purchases, please contact Sterling Special Sales Department at 800-805-5489 or specialsales@sterlingpub.com.

Contents

Don Hanson III
Hanson Mastersmith Quillon Dagger | 2007

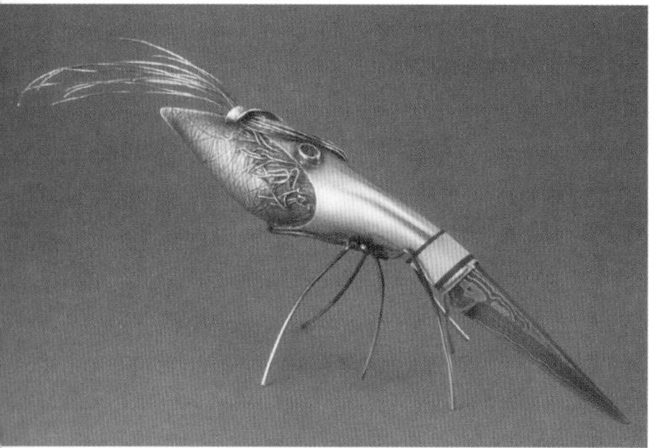

Chantal Gilbert
Mademoiselle | 2001

Introduction

To create art from an object that is primarily defined by its associations—many of which have to do with violence and aggression—is a complex and fascinating task. It's an exercise in pushing boundaries. The knife has long been both feared and revered, and I believe that these qualities are part of what make it a medium worth exploring.

This book boldly proclaims that in the hands of skilled artisans, knives can transcend stereotypes. I believe that this is a historic volume, one that will prove to be an important step in the acceptance of the knife as a legitimate art form. The knifemakers of today use materials and methods both old and new. They are true pioneers, and I am excited about sharing their work with you.

The tradition of creating ornamental edged weaponry is a strong one, and radical steps are being taken in thousands of artist studios around the world to expand and transform that tradition. Flip through these pages, and you'll discover a dizzying array of styles, forms, and creative interpretations: daggers, hunting knives, combat and folding knives, switchblades and multi-blades, swords, axes, tomahawks, kitchen knives—even a pistol-knife. You'll see pieces that transcend form and function to become sculptural works of art. You'll see knives that are raw and knives that are refined, knives that demonstrate simple elegance, and knives that feature over-the-top embellishment.

Many of the pieces in this book were produced by the members of a little-known art movement—a group of talented craftsmen largely unrecognized by the general public. My goal over the years has been to bridge this special movement with the mainstream art and jewelry worlds and to expand the public's perception of what a knife can be. Through this volume, I'm sure you'll discover why it is that I and so many others have chosen the knife as our medium.

Artists like Don Hanson and Tim Hancock create daggers that are modern interpretations of classic forms, while Rebecca Scheer and Chantal Gilbert use their work as an outlet for wit and commentary.

Anders Högström combines the aesthetics of several different cultures into one style of knife to create an entirely new form, such as Euro-Persian or Nordic-Samurai. Vince Evans is a master of historically accurate reproductions, and Frankie Flood produces tricked-out pizza cutters.

Incorporating vivid tints through anodized titanium and chemically colored steels, contemporary knifemakers are far more daring than their counterparts from even a generation ago. With his unique mosaics, Swedish artist Johan Gustafsson is producing Damascus steel patterns the samurai never dreamed of. Combining form and function in his innovative art-utility knives, Allen Elishewitz uses unique materials like meteorite and titanium, as well as an old decorative art known as *guilloché*.

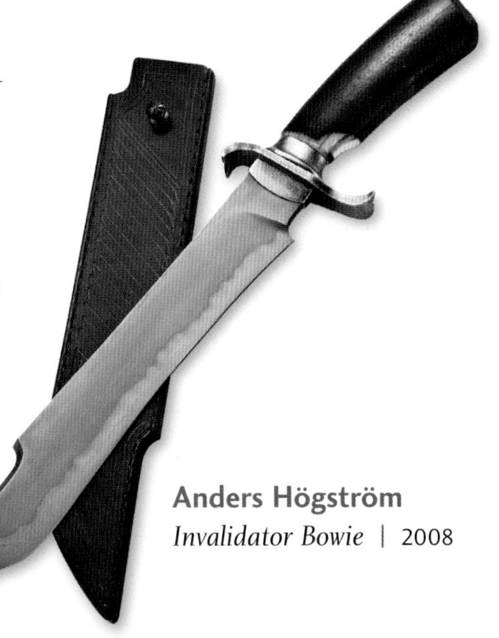

Anders Högström
Invalidator Bowie | 2008

Although they're still creating one of mankind's earliest tools, contemporary knifemakers are the masters of new techniques and technologies. Computer-aided design (CAD) and computer-aided manufacturing (CAM) enable modern knife artists to produce multiples and complex designs in shorter periods of time. Laser and water-jet cutting are used to make intricate parts and fittings. New advancements in Damascus steel have been made possible through the use of electrical discharge machining (EDM) and powder metallurgy, which can be used to create shapes and images that seem to come alive in steel. Yet—no matter how technologically advanced we makers become—the knife always returns us to the traditions of our ancient ancestors. The true lure of knifemaking is that it allows for modern interpretations of a classic form.

This collection features a broad range of work from some of the finest knifemakers in the field today, including legendary craftsmen and artists who are less well known. I hope that their work inspires further exploration of the knife as a creative form. I look forward to participating in the development of this dynamic medium and to the exciting possibilities the future holds. Selecting the knives featured here was a pleasure and a privilege, and I am proud to present them to you.

John L. Jensen, Juror

Tim Hancock
Dog-Bone Dagger #1 | 2005

Curt Erickson

Art Dagger | 2006

OVERALL LENGTH, 15 INCHES (38.1 CM)

Dendritic agate, gold, platinum; engraved, inlaid

GOLD, PLATINUM, AND ENGRAVING BY JULIE WARENSKI-ERICKSON
PHOTO BY JIM COOPER OF SHARPBYCOOP.COM

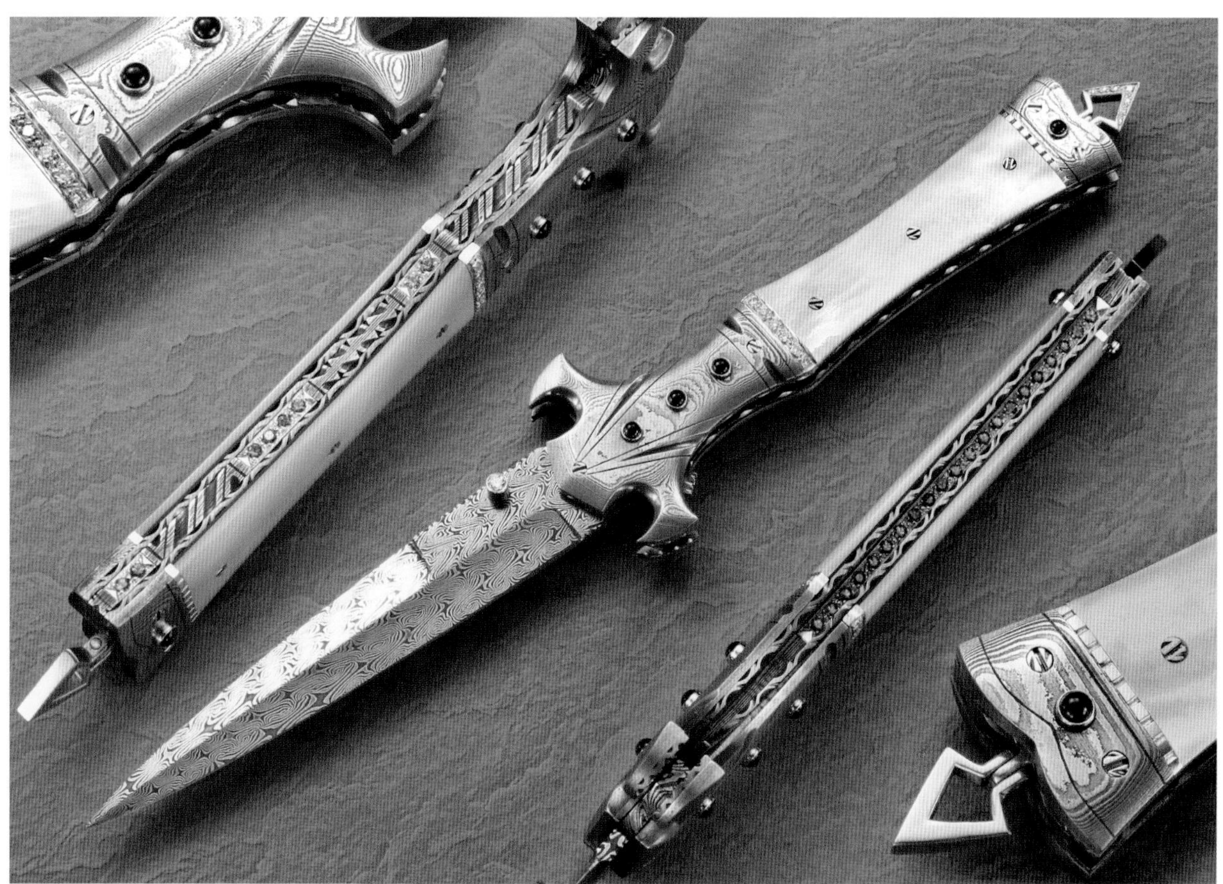

George E. Dailey

Charisma | 1998

OVERALL LENGTH, 10 INCHES (25.4 CM)

Turkish twist Damascus steel, diamonds, black onyx, 14-karat gold, gold-lip mother-of-pearl, titanium; set, anodized

DAMASCUS STEEL BY DARYL MEIER
PHOTO BY JIM COOPER OF SHARPBYCOOP.COM

Stan Wilson

Untitled | 2007

OVERALL LENGTH, 7 5/16 INCHES (18.6 CM)

Twist Damascus steel, black-lip pearl, white diamonds, titanium; file worked, jeweled, anodized

DAMASCUS STEEL BY DEVIN THOMAS
PHOTO BY JIM COOPER OF SHARPBYCOOP.COM

Owen Wood

Folding Boot Knife | 2006

OVERALL LENGTH, 6¾ INCHES (17.1 CM)

Herringbone and explosion composite Damascus steel, 416 stainless steel, 303 stainless steel, black-lip pearl, titanium; engraved, inlaid

ENGRAVED BY TIM GEORGE
PHOTO BY JIM COOPER OF SHARPBYCOOP.COM

Ken Steigerwalt

Persian Dagger | 2007

BLADE, 6 1/2 INCHES (16.5 CM)

Damascus steel, 440C stainless steel, pin shell, 18-karat gold; inlaid, integral constructed

DAMASCUS STEEL BY MIKE NORRIS
PHOTO BY JIM COOPER OF SHARPBYCOOP.COM

Van Barnett
Folding Dagger: Impact | 2002
OVERALL LENGTH, 11 INCHES (28 CM)
Rolling river Damascus steel, 14-karat yellow gold, 24-karat gold, mother-of-pearl, rubies, titanium; forged, etched, carved, engraved, inlaid, file worked
PHOTO BY POINTSEVEN STUDIOS

Shane Taylor
The Reign of Evil | 2005
$4^{1}/_{8}$ X $^{9}/_{16}$ X $^{3}/_{16}$ INCHES (10.5 X 1.5 X 0.5 CM)
Mosaic Damascus steel, mammoth ivory, 24-karat gold; carved, inlaid, sculpted
PHOTO BY POINTSEVEN STUDIOS

Fred Carter

Untitled | Mid-1980s

OVERALL LENGTH, 14 INCHES (35.6 CM)

O1 steel, mild steel, 24-karat gold; engraved

PHOTO BY JIM COOPER OF SHARPBYCOOP.COM

Johnny Stout

The Protégé | 2005

$^{15}/_{16}$ X $^{9}/_{16}$ X $7^{11}/_{16}$ INCHES (2.4 X 1.4 X 19.5 CM)

Ladder-pattern Damascus steel, mammoth ivory; engraved

DAMASCUS STEEL BY JERRY RADOS
ENGRAVED BY JIM SMALL
PHOTO BY JIM COOPER OF SHARPBYCOOP.COM

Andy Shinosky

Untitled | 2007

OVERALL LENGTH, 7 INCHES (17.8 CM)

Damascus steel, stainless steel, gold anodized titanium; liner-lock design, engraved

PHOTO BY ARTIST

Don Hanson III

Hanson Stag Hunter | 2005

OVERALL LENGTH, 9 13/16 INCHES (25 CM)

1086 steel, mosaic Damascus steel, hamon, amber stag; forged

PHOTO BY JIM COOPER OF SHARPBYCOOP.COM

Steve E. Hill

El Diablo | 2006

OVERALL LENGTH, 12 13/16 INCHES (32.5 CM)

Braided Damascus steel, mammoth ivory; carved, textured, heat colored, sculpted

PHOTO BY POINTSEVEN STUDIOS

Joe Szilaski

Mountain-Eagle Pipe Tomahawk | 2007

HEAD, $7^1/_4$ INCHES (18.4 CM)

W-2 tool steel, silver wire, bird's-eye maple; forged, heat-treated, carved, inlaid, engraved

PHOTO BY LORI SZILASKI

Don Hanson III

Artifact Bowie #2 | 2007

OVERALL LENGTH, 19 INCHES (48.3 CM)

Hanson W-2 tool steel, Hanson Damascus steel, vivid hamon, fossil walrus ivory; forged

PHOTO BY JIM COOPER OF SHARPBYCOOP.COM

Arpád Bojtoš
Hommage à Bruno Bruni | 2007
OVERALL LENGTH, 11 13/16 INCHES (30 CM)
440C stainless steel, mammoth ivory, ebony, silver, gold
PHOTO BY JULIUS MOJZIS

Vladimir Burkovski

The Goddess | 1997

6 15/16 X 1 5/16 X 15/16 INCHES (17.7 X 3.4 X 2.4 CM)

Carbon steel, sterling silver, pre-1966 sperm whale tooth, mammoth tooth, silver, mother-of-pearl; cast, engraved, carved, incrusted

PHOTOS BY DR. DAVID DAROM

Tommy McNabb

Damascus Chief | 2006

OVERALL LENGTH, 11 INCHES (27.9 CM)

Damascus steel, nickel silver, stag handle; carved, welded

PHOTOS BY TERRILL HOFFMAN PHOTOGRAPHY

George E. Dailey

Indian | 2003

OVERALL LENGTH, 5 1/2 INCHES (14 CM)

416 stainless steel, diamonds, 18-karat gold, mother-of-pearl; inlaid, engraved

ENGRAVED BY RAY COVER, JR.
STEEL BY GARY HOUSE
PHOTO BY JIM COOPER OF SHARPBYCOOP.COM

George E. Dailey

Vikings | 2002

OVERALL LENGTH, 9 INCHES (22.9 CM)

Damascus steel, diamonds, 18-karat yellow gold, 18-karat rose gold, black-lip mother-of-pearl; engraved

DAMASCUS STEEL BY CONNY PERSSON
ENGRAVED BY RAY COVER, JR.
PHOTO BY JIM COOPER OF SHARPBYCOOP.COM

Scott Sawby

Shearwater | 2004

OVERALL LENGTH, $6^{1}/_{16}$ INCHES (15.4 CM)

ATS-34 steel, 416 stainless steel, black-lip mother-of-pearl; inlaid, engraved

ENGRAVED BY RAY COVER, JR.
PHOTO BY JIM COOPER OF SHARPBYCOOP.COM

Gail Lunn

Triple Play | 2008

OVERALL LENGTH, $8^{1}/2$ INCHES (21.6 CM)

Dragon-skin Damascus steel, ladder-pattern Damascus steel, black-lip pearl, sapphires, gold

PHOTO BY JIM COOPER OF SHARPBYCOOP.COM

John L. Jensen

Syndrome | 2007

OVERALL LENGTH, 8½ INCHES (21.6 CM)

Accordioned mosaic Damascus steel, explosion composite Damascus steel, titanium, 18-karat royal yellow gold, peridot, garnets, sapphires, blue paua shell, abalone, citrine; hollow ground, etched, hot blued, chemically colored

PHOTO BY JESSICA MARCOTTE

Jack Levin

Don Quixote | 2003

OVERALL LENGTH, 10 INCHES (25.4 CM)

Tool steel, stainless steel, 24-karat gold, spring steel; blued, carved

PHOTO BY ARTIST

Warren Osborne

Model 33 Dagger | 2000

OVERALL LENGTH, 6 1/8 INCHES (15.6 CM)

Stainless Damascus steel, 416 stainless steel, black-lip mother-of-pearl; inlaid

DAMASCUS STEEL BY MIKE NORRIS
PHOTO BY JIM COOPER OF SHARPBYCOOP.COM

Jot Singh Khalsa

Fancy Embellished Kirpan | 2006

OVERALL LENGTH, 13¾ INCHES (34.9 CM)

Stainless Damascus steel, ocean jasper, sterling silver, fine diamonds, green tourmaline, 24-karat gold; engraved, inlaid, set

ENGRAVED, INLAID, AND SET BY JULIE WARENSKI-ERICKSON
PHOTO BY JIM COOPER OF SHARPBYCOOP.COM

Curt Erickson

Art Dagger | 2007

BLADE, 6 INCHES (15.2 CM)

ATS-34 steel, antique elephant ivory, nickel silver; carved, engraved

ENGRAVED BY JULIE WARENSKI-ERICKSON
PHOTO BY JIM COOPER OF SHARPBYCOOP.COM

Owen Wood

Art Nouveau Folding Knife | 2008

OVERALL LENGTH, 4¾ INCHES (12.1 CM)

Pinstripe and explosion Damascus steel, stainless Damascus steel, 303 stainless steel, 416 stainless steel, titanium; blued, engraved

ENGRAVED BY AMAYAK STEPANYAN
PHOTO BY JIM COOPER OF SHARPBYCOOP.COM

Edmund Davidson

The Orgasmatron | 2007

OVERALL LENGTH, 20¼ INCHES (51.4 CM)

440C stainless steel, box elder; engraved, heat-treated, integral constructed

ENGRAVED BY JERE DAVIDSON
HEAT-TREATED BY PAUL BOS
PHOTO BY POINTSEVEN STUDIOS

Rick Eaton

Persian Window Frame—Flowering Damascus | 2006

BLADE, 3 1/2 INCHES (8.9 CM)

Damascus steel, nickel, 24-karat gold, black-lip pearl; engraved

PHOTO BY POINTSEVEN STUDIOS

Dennis E. Friedly

The Long-Stem Bowie | 2006

OVERALL LENGTH, $14\frac{15}{16}$ INCHES (38 CM)

440C stainless steel, 416 stainless steel, fossil walrus ivory; fluted, engraved, carved

ENGRAVED BY GIL RUDOLPH
PHOTOS BY POINTSEVEN STUDIOS

Johnny Stout

The Zodiac | 2006

OVERALL LENGTH, 7⁵⁄₈ INCHES (19.4 CM)

Feather-pattern Damascus steel, mosaic Damascus steel; engraved

FEATHER-PATTERN DAMASCUS STEEL BY ARTIST AND HARVEY DEAN
MOSAIC DAMASCUS STEEL BY ROBERT EGGERLING
ENGRAVED BY JIM SMALL
PHOTO BY JIM COOPER OF SHARPBYCOOP.COM

Josef Rusňák
Buddy Weston

Life II | 2004

OVERALL LENGTH, 5¾ INCHES (14.5 CM)

Stainless Damascus steel, gold, silver, titanium; carved

PHOTO BY JIM COOPER OF SHARPBYCOOP.COM

Koji Hara

Zen | 2001

OVERALL LENGTH, 5 11/16 INCHES (14.5 CM)

Cowry-Y steel, 420 stainless steel, mother-of-pearl; carved, inlaid, polished

PHOTO BY JIM COOPER OF SHARPBYCOOP.COM

E. Jay Hendrickson

Long-Clip Trailing-Point Bowie | 2007

OVERALL LENGTH, 15 INCHES (38.1 CM); BLADE, 10 INCHES (25.4 CM)

5160 steel, curly maple, fine silver, nickel silver, ivory; inlaid, file worked, carved, engraved

PHOTO BY POINTSEVEN STUDIOS

Anders Högström

Khyber/Jambiya | 2007

OVERALL LENGTH, 25 3/8 INCHES (64.5 CM)

Hanson Damascus steel, bronze, copper, jet, leather; antiqued, textured, inlaid

PHOTO BY JIM COOPER OF SHARPBYCOOP.COM

Don Hanson III

Hanson Mastersmith Quillon Dagger | 2007

OVERALL LENGTH, 18 INCHES (45.7 CM)

Hanson Damascus steel, fossil walrus ivory, 22-karat rose gold; forged, fluted, twisted, inlaid

PHOTO BY JIM COOPER OF SHARPBYCOOP.COM

Anders Högström

Kasbah Persian | 2008

BLADE, 11 13/16 INCHES (30 CM)

1050 steel, walrus, bronze, buffalo horn; clay tempered

PHOTO BY JIM COOPER OF SHARPBYCOOP.COM

David Broadwell

Persian | 2000

OVERALL LENGTH, 11 13/16 INCHES (30 CM)

Damascus steel, curly koa, 14-karat gold

PHOTO BY JIM COOPER OF SHARPBYCOOP.COM

MICKE (Michael Andersson)

Untitled | 2007

17 11/16 X 2 3/8 X 5/16 INCHES (45 X 6 X 0.8 CM)

Mosaic Damascus steel, mammoth ivory; forge welded

PHOTO BY ANDRÉ ANDERSSON

Russ Andrews II

Lombardo Bowie | 2006

OVERALL LENGTH, $20\frac{7}{8}$ INCHES (53 CM)

W-2 steel, twist Damascus steel, amboyna burl; forged

PHOTO BY JIM COOPER OF SHARPBYCOOP.COM

Don Polzien

Untitled | 2007

OVERALL LENGTH, 19¼ INCHES (49 CM)

Damascus steel, sterling silver, bronze, wood; hand carved, lacquered

PHOTO BY TERRILL HOFFMAN

Jody Muller

Oriental Warrior | 2006

OVERALL LENGTH, $10^{1}/_{4}$ INCHES (26 CM)

Nickel-composite Damascus steel, mosaic Damascus steel, mammoth ivory; sculpted, hand engraved

PHOTO BY JIM COOPER OF SHARPBYCOOP.COM

David Broadwell

The Yamane Knife | 2006

OVERALL LENGTH, 15 INCHES (38.1 CM)

Mosaic Damascus steel, ebony, bronze, sterling silver, oak

PHOTO BY JIM COOPER OF SHARPBYCOOP.COM

Paul M. Jarvis

Copper Nickel Silver Bali Song | 2002

OVERALL LENGTH, 8 INCHES (20.3 CM)

Copper, nickel silver, garnets; carved, set

PHOTO BY JIM COOPER OF SHARPBYCOOP.COM

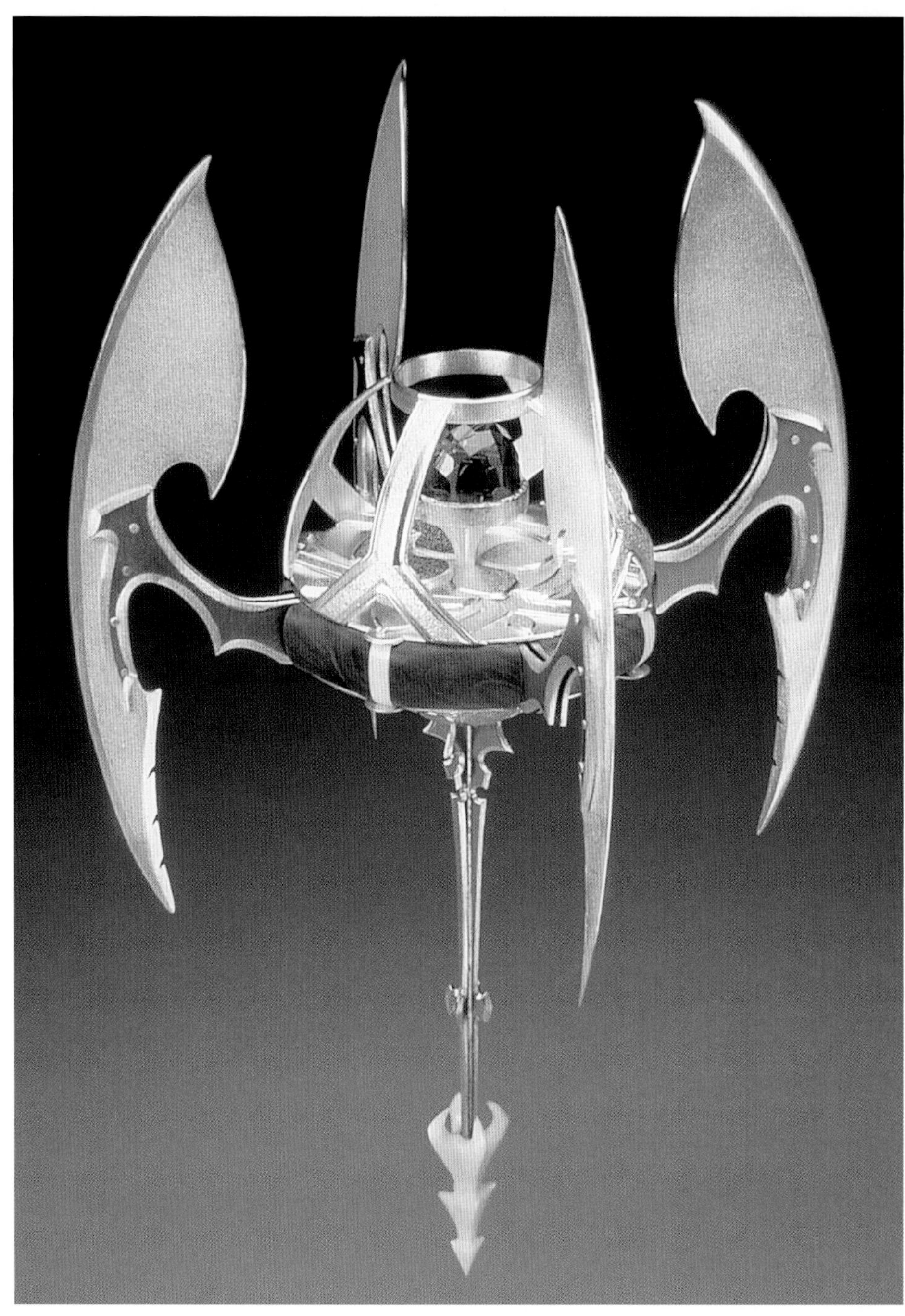

Tom Ferrero

Gourd Knife | 2007

11 X 7 1/16 X 7 1/16 INCHES
(28 X 18 X 18 CM)

Silver, 22-karat gold, amethyst, bone, walnut, patina; hand fabricated, roller printed, stamped, riveted, carved

PHOTO BY KEVIN MONTAGUE

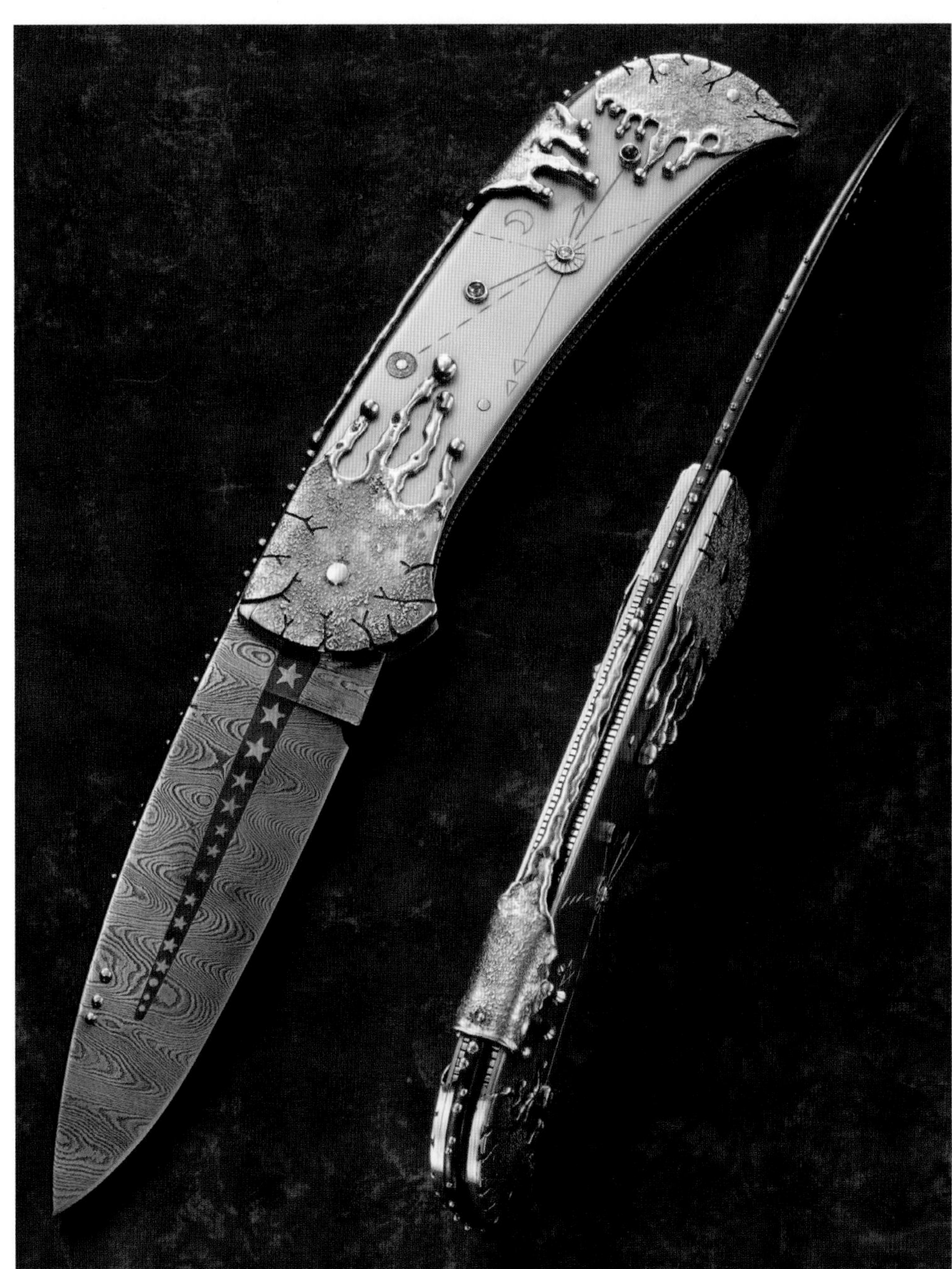

Dellana

Lock-Back Folder: Big Magic | 2005

1 3/8 X 8 3/8 X 3/8 INCHES
(3.5 X 21.3 X 1 CM)

Composite Damascus steel, 14-karat yellow, rose, and green gold, 22-karat gold, diamonds, rubies, tanzanites; forged, etched, fabricated, fused, bead blasted, engraved, file worked

PHOTO BY POINTSEVEN STUDIOS

Ronald Best

Untitled | 2008

OVERALL LENGTH, 13 INCHES (33 CM)

440C stainless steel, madrone burl; engraved

ENGRAVED BY JERE DAVIDSON
PHOTO BY JIM COOPER OF SHARPBYCOOP.COM

Shane Taylor

Night Wing | 2007

$2^{3}/_{4}$ X $^{3}/_{8}$ X $^{3}/_{16}$ INCHES (7 X 1 X 0.5 CM)

Image mosaic Damascus, mammoth ivory, walrus ivory, gold; carved, sculpted, engraved

PHOTO BY POINTSEVEN STUDIOS

Ron Newton

Shootin' Newton Gun Bowie | 2003

4 X 3/4 X 15 INCHES (10.2 X 1.9 X 38.1 CM)

High-carbon steel, steel, checkered ebony, abalone, 24-karat gold; blued, engraved, inlaid

PHOTO BY POINTSEVEN STUDIOS

R.J. Martin

Avenger and *Contender Flippers* | 2003

AVENGER (TOP), OVERALL LENGTH, $9\frac{7}{16}$ INCHES (24 CM);
CONTENDER (BOTTOM), OVERALL LENGTH, $7\frac{7}{16}$ INCHES (19 CM)

CPM-S30V steel, G-10 steel, titanium

PHOTO BY JIM COOPER OF SHARPBYCOOP.COM

David Broadwell

Fantasy Warriors | 2008

OVERALL LENGTH, 7 1/16 INCHES (18 CM)

Mosaic Damascus steel, stainless steel, titanium

PHOTO BY JIM COOPER OF SHARPBYCOOP.COM

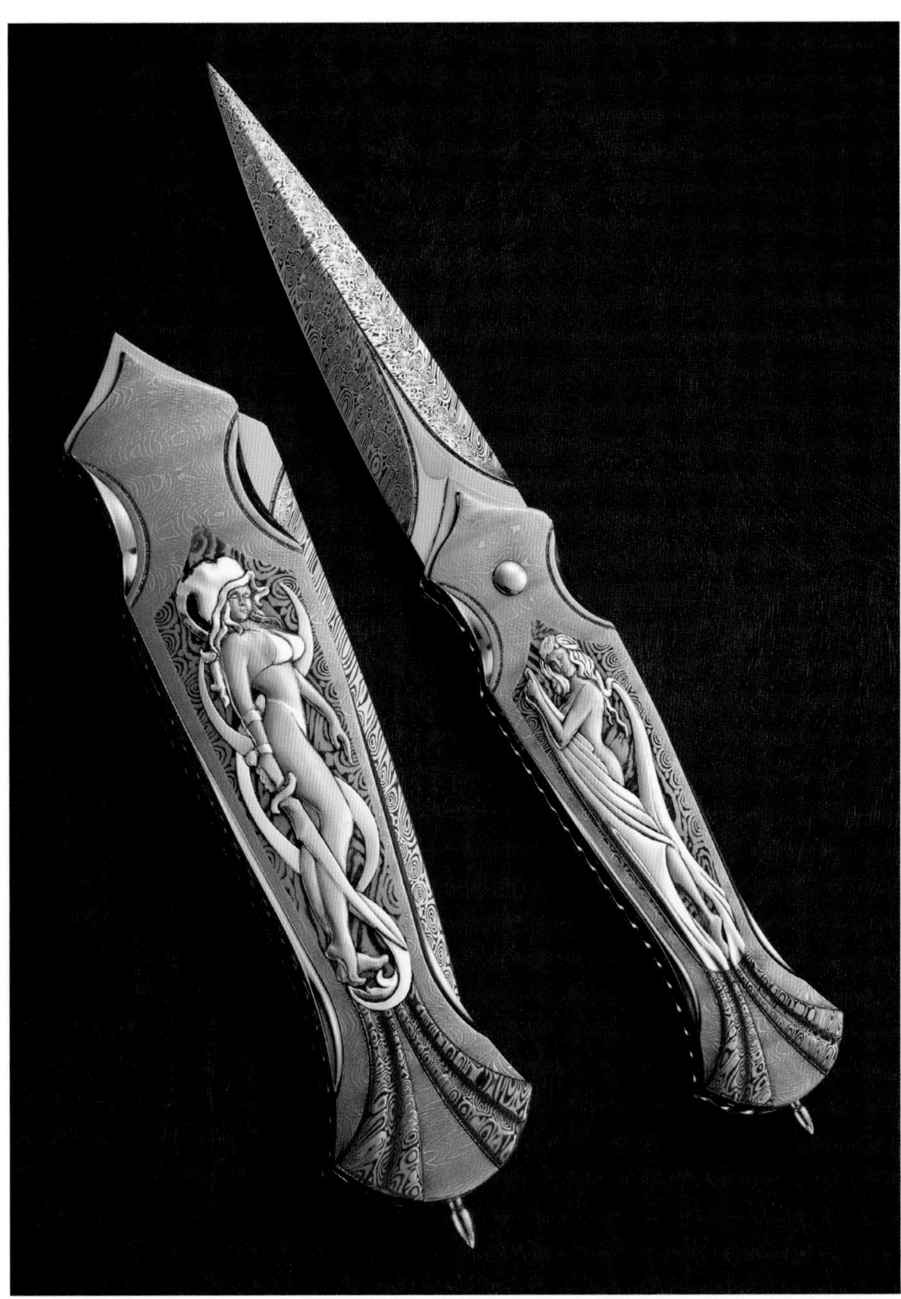

Matthew Lerch

Paia Dagger | 2007

OVERALL LENGTH, 8 1/2 INCHES (21.6 CM)

Stainless Damascus steel, Damascus, sterling silver, 24-karat gold; engraved

ENGRAVED BY RON SKAGGS
PHOTO BY JIM COOPER OF SHARPBYCOOP.COM

Keith Ouye

Dead Man's Chest | 2007

OVERALL LENGTH, 8 5/8 INCHES (21.9 CM)

S30V stainless steel, 6AL4V titanium; engraved, heat-treated

ENGRAVED BY C.J. CAI
HEAT-TREATED BY PAUL BOS
PHOTO BY JIM COOPER OF SHARPBYCOOP.COM

Bill Saindon

Grim Reaper: Pushbutton Release Side-Lock Symmetrical Dagger | 2004

OVERALL LENGTH, 10 INCHES (25.4 CM)

Damascus steel, 416 stainless steel, fossil walrus ivory, titanium, gold; carved, file worked, engraved, inlaid

DAMASCUS STEEL BY GARY HOUSE
ENGRAVED AND INLAID BY RAY COVER, JR.
PHOTO BY JIM COOPER OF SHARPBYCOOP.COM

Steve E. Hill

La Catrina | 2007

OVERALL LENGTH, 9 3/16 INCHES (23.4 CM)

Braided Damascus steel, twist Damascus steel, black mammoth ivory; file worked, carved

PHOTO BY POINTSEVEN STUDIOS

Don Hanson III

Fossil Fighter | 2007

OVERALL LENGTH, 11 INCHES (28 CM)

Mosaic Damascus steel, fossil walrus ivory, 18-karat rose gold, titanium; forged, inlaid, file worked

PHOTO BY JIM COOPER OF SHARPBYCOOP.COM

Brian Tighe

Tighe One On | 2007

BLADE, 3 5/8 INCHES (9.2 CM)

Stainless Damascus steel, black-lip mother-of-pearl; fluted, inlaid

PHOTO BY POINTSEVEN STUDIOS

Pat Crawford
Wes Crawford

Wooly Triumph | 2007

OVERALL LENGTH, $9\frac{1}{2}$ INCHES (24 CM)

Stainless Damascus steel, titanium, wooly mammoth bark ivory, sapphires; file worked, engine turned

PHOTO BY JIM COOPER OF SHARPBYCOOP.COM

Kaj Embretsen

Drop-Point Back-Lock Folder | 2008

Damascus steel, mammoth ivory, gold

PHOTO BY JIM COOPER OF SHARPBYCOOP.COM

Cliff Parker

Untitled | 2005

OVERALL LENGTH, 6 $^{11}/_{16}$ INCHES (17 CM)

Mosaic Damascus steel, fossil walrus ivory; file worked

PHOTO BY JIM COOPER OF SHARPBYCOOP.COM

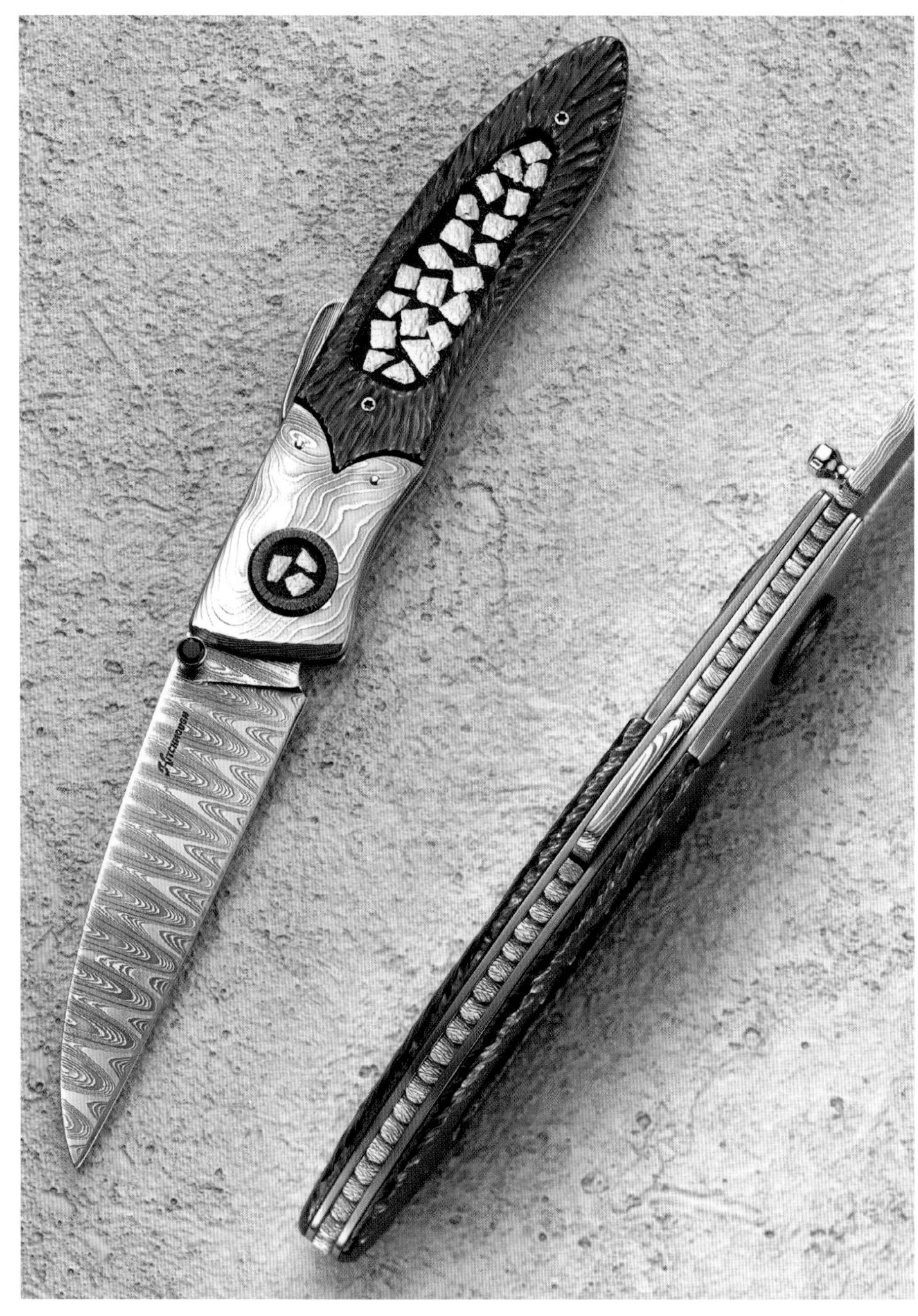

Howard Hitchmough
Goldrush | 2003
OVERALL LENGTH, 7 1/4 INCHES (18.5 CM)
Stainless Damascus steel, 24-karat gold, titanium, 18-karat gold, sapphire
PHOTO BY POINTSEVEN STUDIOS

Cliff Parker

Untitled | 2005

OVERALL LENGTH, 6 11/16 INCHES (17 CM)

Mosaic Damascus steel, fossil walrus ivory; file worked

PHOTO BY JIM COOPER OF SHARPBYCOOP.COM

Des Horn

Folding Knife with Small Inter-Frame Back Lock | 2007

OVERALL LENGTH, 5 5/16 INCHES (13.5 CM); BLADE, 2 7/16 INCHES (6.2 CM)

Stainless Damascus steel, 416 stainless steel, Gibeon meteorite, 24-karat gold; double tempered, cryogenically treated, inlaid, engraved

ENGRAVED BY ARMIN WINKLER
PHOTO BY JIM COOPER OF SHARPBYCOOP.COM

William Henry Studio

T10 Lancet | 1997–2006

OVERALL LENGTH, 6 INCHES (15.2 CM)

Raindrop Damascus steel, pearl, rubies; carved, inset

PHOTO BY JIM COOPER OF SHARPBYCOOP.COM

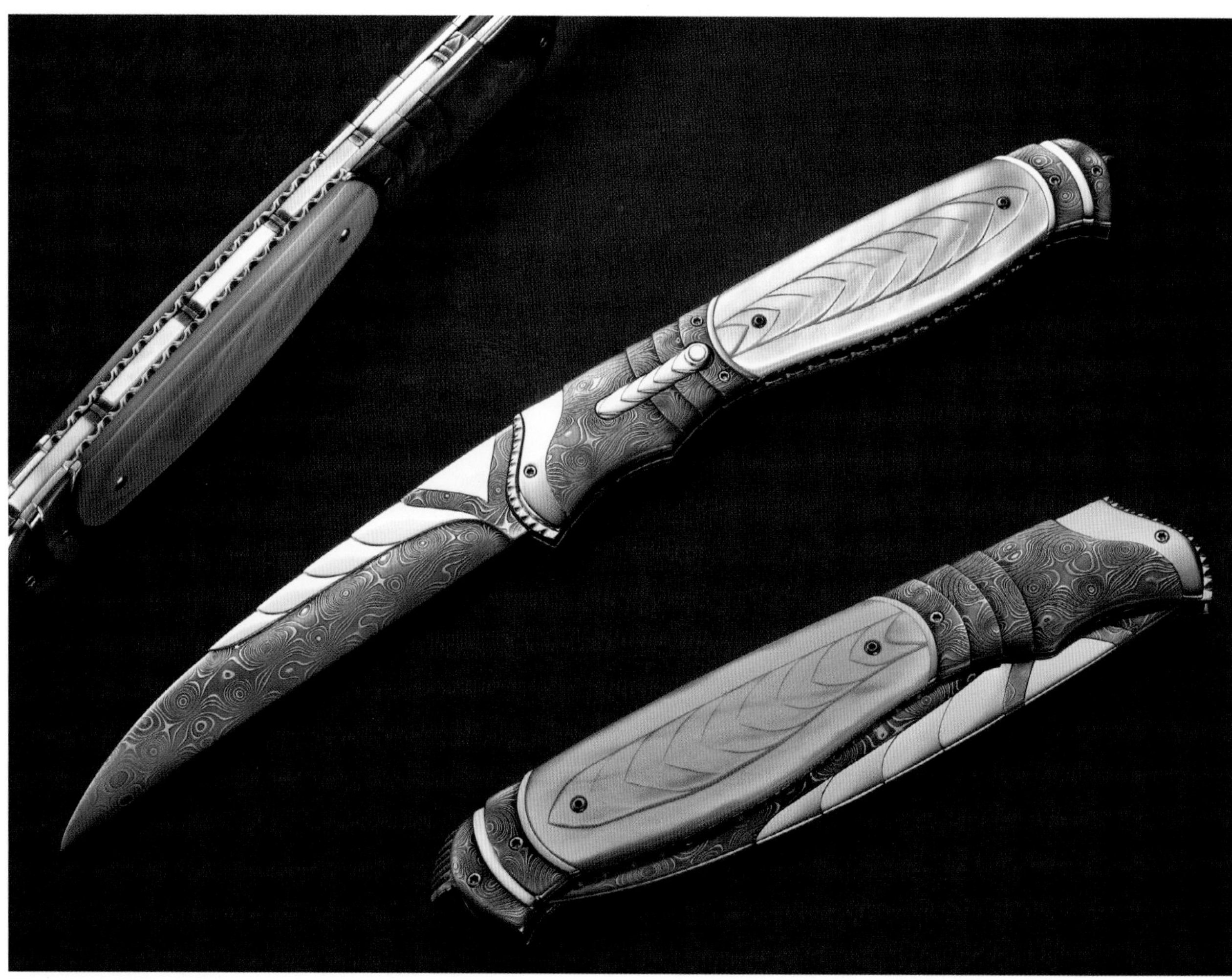

Rex R. Robinson

Retribution | 2007

OVERALL LENGTH, 10 INCHES (25.4 CM)

Damascus steel, titanium

DAMASCUS STEEL BY DEVIN THOMAS
PHOTO BY JIM COOPER OF SHARPBYCOOP.COM

Jack Levin

Roman-Style Folding Dagger | 1995

OVERALL LENGTH, 7¾ INCHES (19.7 CM)

Damascus steel, ATS-34 steel, titanium, 24-karat gold, mother-of-pearl

PHOTO BY JIM COOPER OF SHARPBYCOOP.COM

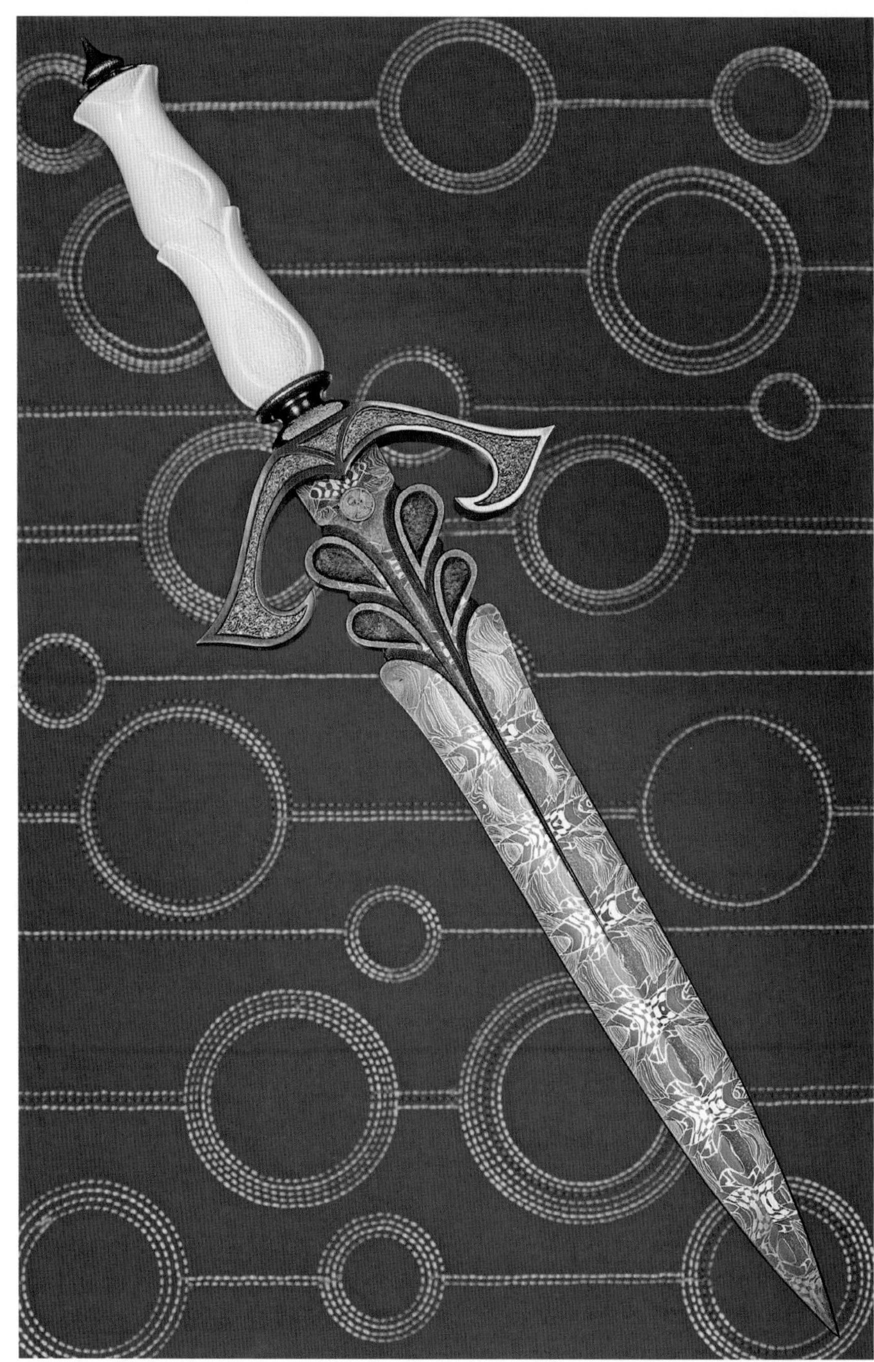

Peter Mason

Phantom Dagger | 2007

16 1/8 X 4 11/16 X 1 3/16 INCHES
(41 X 12 X 3 CM)

Mosaic Damascus steel, bronze, elephant ivory

BLADE BY ETTORÉ GIANFERRARI
PHOTO BY DORIAN SPENCE

Fred Carter

Untitled | Mid-1980s

OVERALL LENGTH, 14 INCHES (35.6 CM)

O1 steel, mild steel, 24-karat gold; engraved

PHOTO BY JIM COOPER OF SHARPBYCOOP.COM

Matthew Lerch

Paia Dagger | 2007

OVERALL LENGTH, 8½ INCHES (21.6 CM)

Damascus steel, black-lip pearl, 24-karat gold

PHOTO BY JIM COOPER OF SHARPBYCOOP.COM

George E. Dailey

Trick Baby | 2002

OVERALL LENGTH, 9½ INCHES (24.1 CM)

Damascus steel, 14-karat gold, diamonds, rubies, fossil walrus ivory

DAMASCUS STEEL BY DARYL MEIER
PHOTO BY CHET BURRACK STUDIO

Jack Levin

Two Baroque-Style Daggers | 2001

OVERALL LENGTH, 10 INCHES (25.4 CM) EACH

416 stainless steel, 1084 spring steel, diamonds, sapphires, 24-karat gold; fluted, inlaid, engraved

PHOTO BY POINTSEVEN STUDIOS

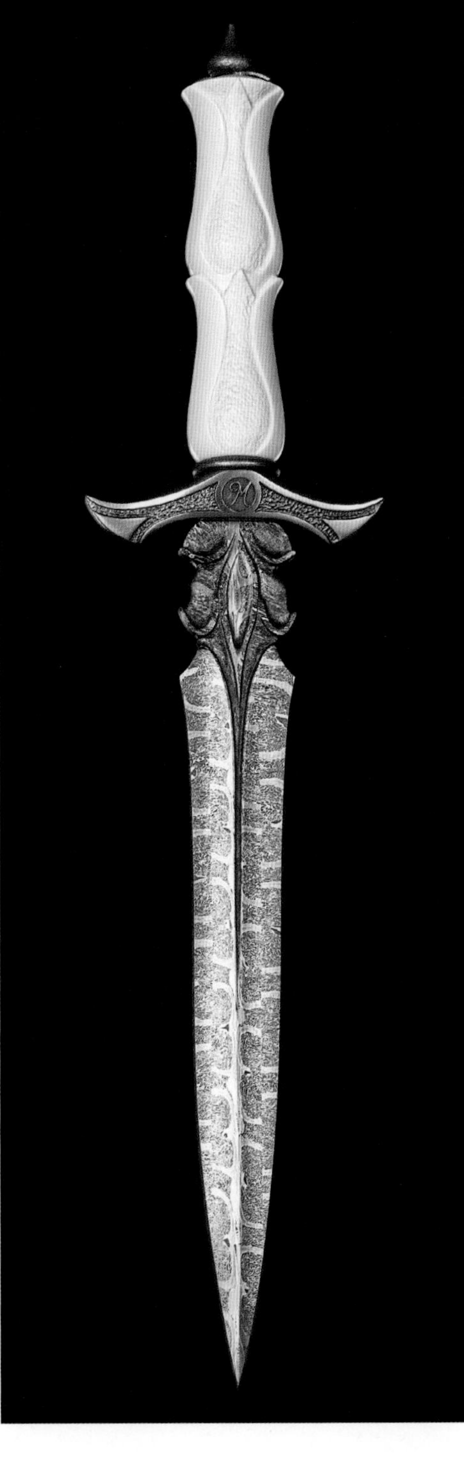

Peter Mason

Highwayman Dagger | 2007

13¾ X 3⁵⁄₁₆ X 1³⁄₁₆ INCHES (35 X 8.5 X 3 CM)

Composite Damascus steel, bronze, elephant ivory

PHOTO BY DORIAN SPENCE

Dellana

Lock-Back Folder:
Love Knife | 2006

1 3/8 X 7 1/4 X 3/8 INCHES
(3.5 X 18.5 X 1 CM)

Composite Damascus steel, 14-karat yellow, rose and green gold, 22-karat gold, diamonds, rubies, emeralds, sapphires, opals; forged, etched, fabricated, textured, engraved, bead blasted, file worked

PHOTO BY POINTSEVEN STUDIOS

Valani (the collaborative team of Van Barnett and Dellana)

Illusion Series: Gold Short Sword/The Scepter | 2007

OVERALL LENGTH, 21 1/16 INCHES (69 CM)

14-karat yellow spring gold, 14-karat yellow gold, 22-karat gold, sterling silver, diamonds, rubies; oxidized, ground, textured, carved, cast, engraved, set

PHOTO BY POINTSEVEN STUDIOS

Gerald E. Corbit

Small Model 9 | 2006

OVERALL LENGTH, 5½ INCHES (14 CM)

Mosaic Damascus steel, black-lip mother-of-pearl, peridots; carved, engraved

DAMASCUS STEEL BY ROBERT EGGERLING
ENGRAVED BY BRUCE SHAW
PHOTO BY JIM COOPER OF SHARPBYCOOP.COM

Jot Singh Khalsa

Sikh Wedding Sword | 2005

OVERALL LENGTH, 42 INCHES (106.7 CM)

Stainless Damascus steel, ocean jasper, gold- and zirconium-plated sterling silver, fine diamonds, green tourmaline, 24-karat gold; inlaid, engraved, set

ENGRAVED AND INLAID BY TIM ADLAM
STONE SETTING BY JULIE WARENSKI-ERICKSON
PHOTO BY POINTSEVEN STUDIOS

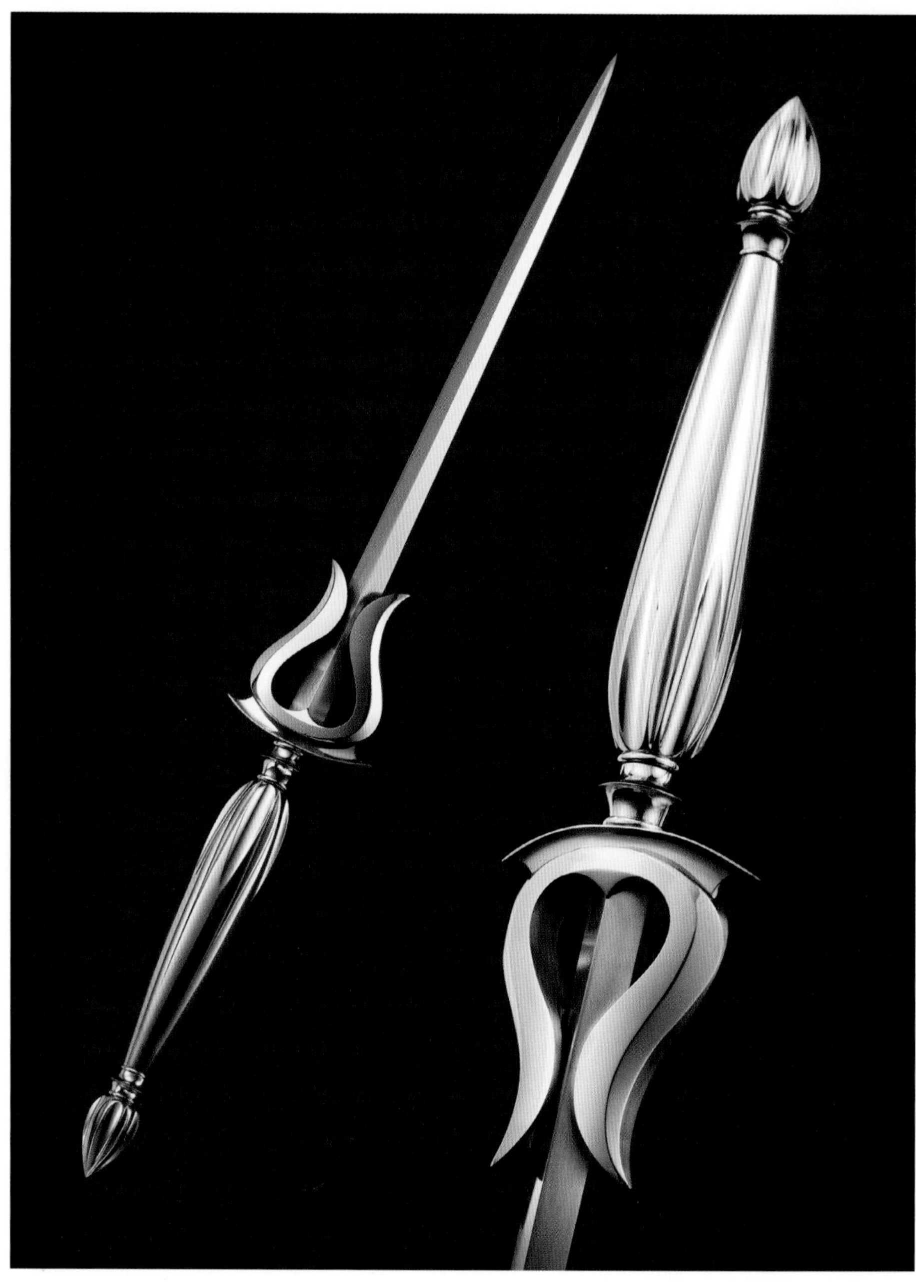

Wolfgang Loerchner
Stainless Steel Stiletto | 1998
OVERALL LENGTH, 11 INCHES (27.9 CM)
440C stainless steel,
316L stainless steel; hand carved
PHOTO BY JIM COOPER OF SHARPBYCOOP.COM

Vince Evans

Scottish Basket Hilt | 2006

OVERALL LENGTH, 39⅜ INCHES (100 CM)

Damascus steel, silver wire, walnut; welded, engraved, inlaid, carved

PHOTO BY POINTSEVEN STUDIOS

Mardi Meshejian

Carved Poinard | 2007

$20^{1}/_{16}$ X 1 X $^{9}/_{16}$ INCHES (51 X 2.5 X 1.5 CM)

Damascus steel; forged, carved, heat colored

PHOTO BY JIM COOPER OF SHARPBYCOOP.COM

Thinus Herbst

Art Folder | 2006

$5^{7}/_{8}$ X $^{3}/_{4}$ X $^{9}/_{16}$ INCHES (15 X 2 X 1.5 CM)

Stainless Damascus steel, mosaic Damascus steel, desert ironwood; file worked

PHOTO BY ARTIST

Jeffrey Cornwell

Serpent | 2008

$9^{7}/_{8}$ X $2^{9}/_{16}$ X $^{1}/_{8}$ INCHES (25.1 X 6.5 X 0.3 CM)

Ladder-pattern Damascus steel; etched

DAMASCUS STEEL BY ROBERT EGGERLING
PHOTO BY JIM COOPER OF SHARPBYCOOP.COM

Kevin King

Spike Kriss | 2007

12½ X ½ INCHES (31.8 X 1.3 CM)

Railroad spike; hand forged, hand twisted

PHOTO BY STEPHEN HILLER

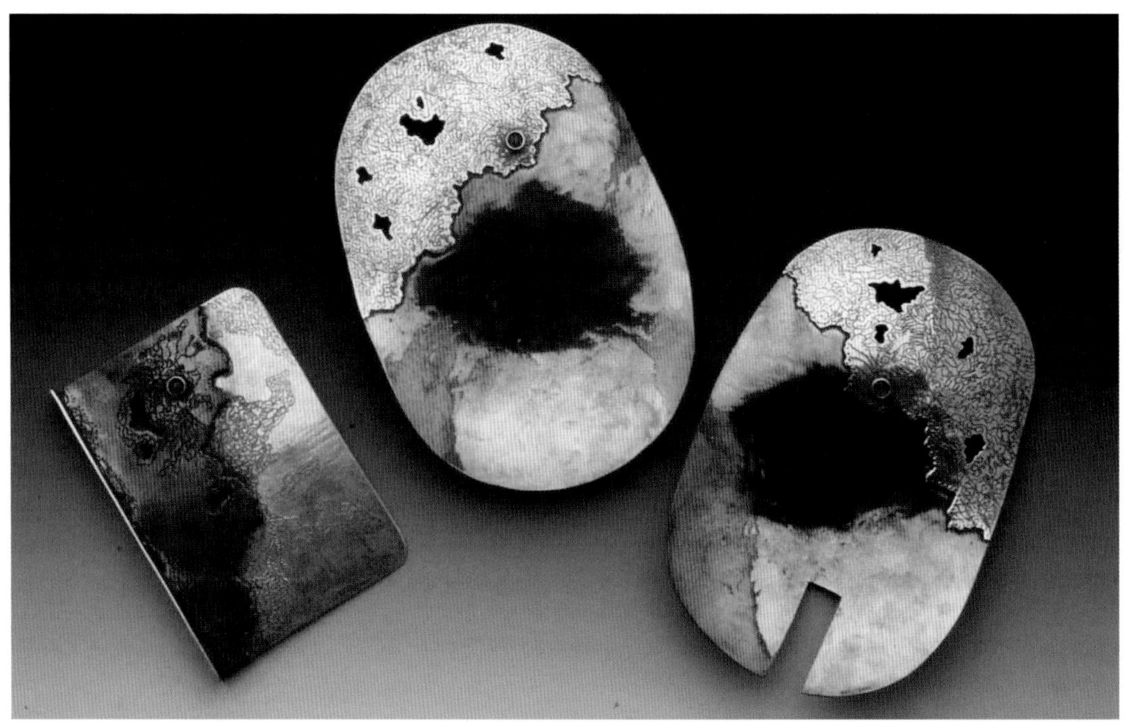

Wendy Jensen McDermott

Untitled | 2000

EACH, 4 INCHES (10.2 CM) LONG

Copper, sterling silver, 14-karat gold, semi-precious stones; engraved, fabricated, formed

PHOTO BY ARTIST

Tom Ferrero

Moss Cutter | 2007

4 11/16 X 8 1/4 X 1 9/16 INCHES (12 X 21 X 4 CM)

Silver, copper, steel, zircon, citrine, tourmaline, afzelia xylay burl; fabricated, etched, riveted, carved

PHOTO BY KEVIN MONTAGUE

John Benjamin Gilliam
Edged Object #9 | 1997
OVERALL LENGTH, 5 INCHES (12.7 CM)
Tool steel, firebrick, epoxy, Corian; cut, ground, etched, carved
PHOTO BY ARTIST

Antoine Van Loocke

Ad Huc Stat | 2001

7⅞ X 9$^{13}/_{16}$ X 9$^{13}/_{16}$ INCHES (20 X 25 X 25 CM)

Damascus steel, water buffalo horn, oosic, wood

PHOTO BY ARTIST

Matthias Lehr

Cradle Knife Silverbronze | 2007

$3\frac{5}{16}$ X $2\frac{3}{8}$ X $\frac{5}{16}$ INCHES (10 X 6 X 0.8 CM)

Bronze; cast

PHOTO BY ARTIST

Gene Michael Pijanowski

Skinner's Knife | 1990

OVERALL LENGTH, $6\frac{11}{16}$ INCHES (17 CM)

Steel, brass, mokume gane; etched

PHOTO BY ARTIST

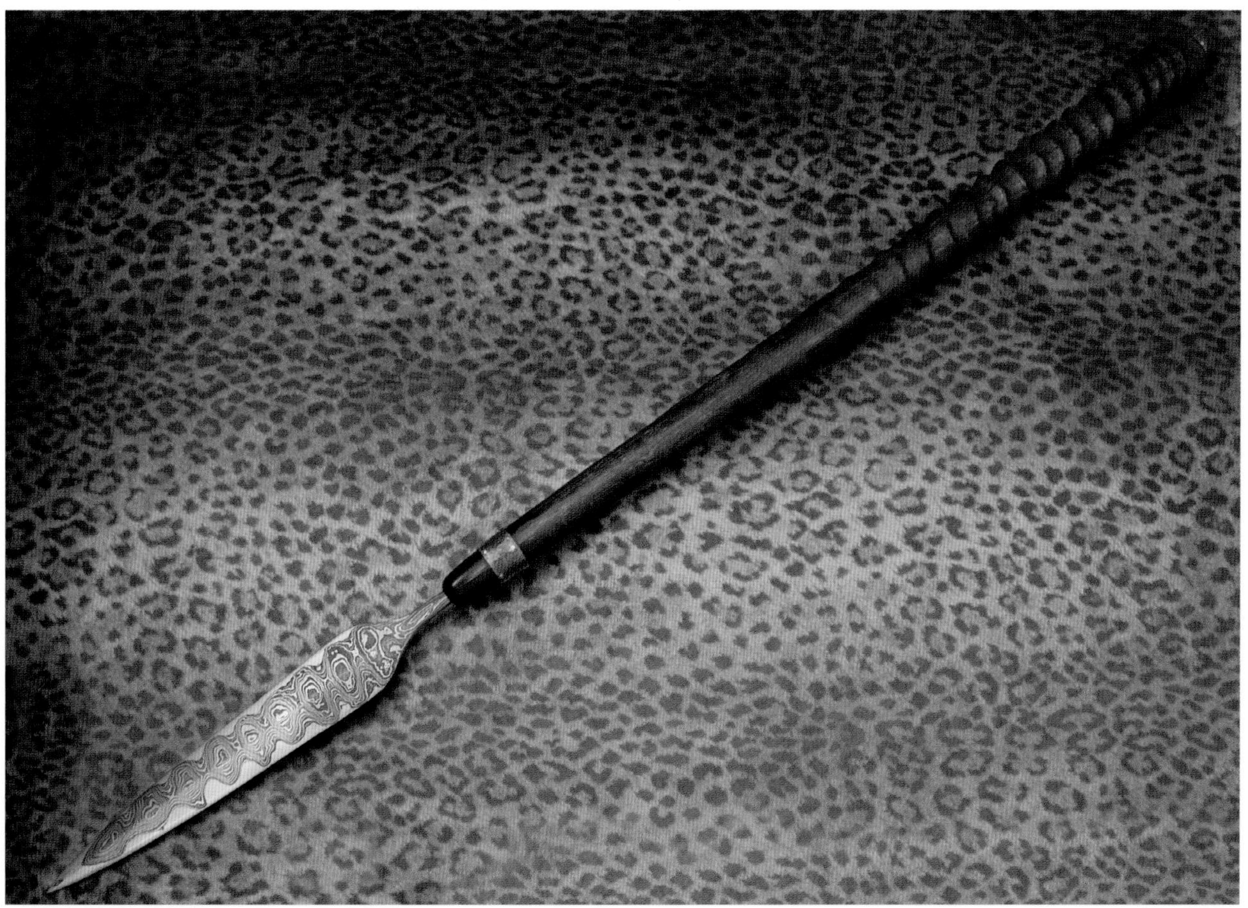

Heather Harvey

Assegai Spear | 2006

OVERALL LENGTH, 36¼ INCHES (92.1 CM)

Carbon steels, gemsbok horn, copper, nickel silver, Swazi coin; forged

PHOTO BY BLADEGALLERY.COM

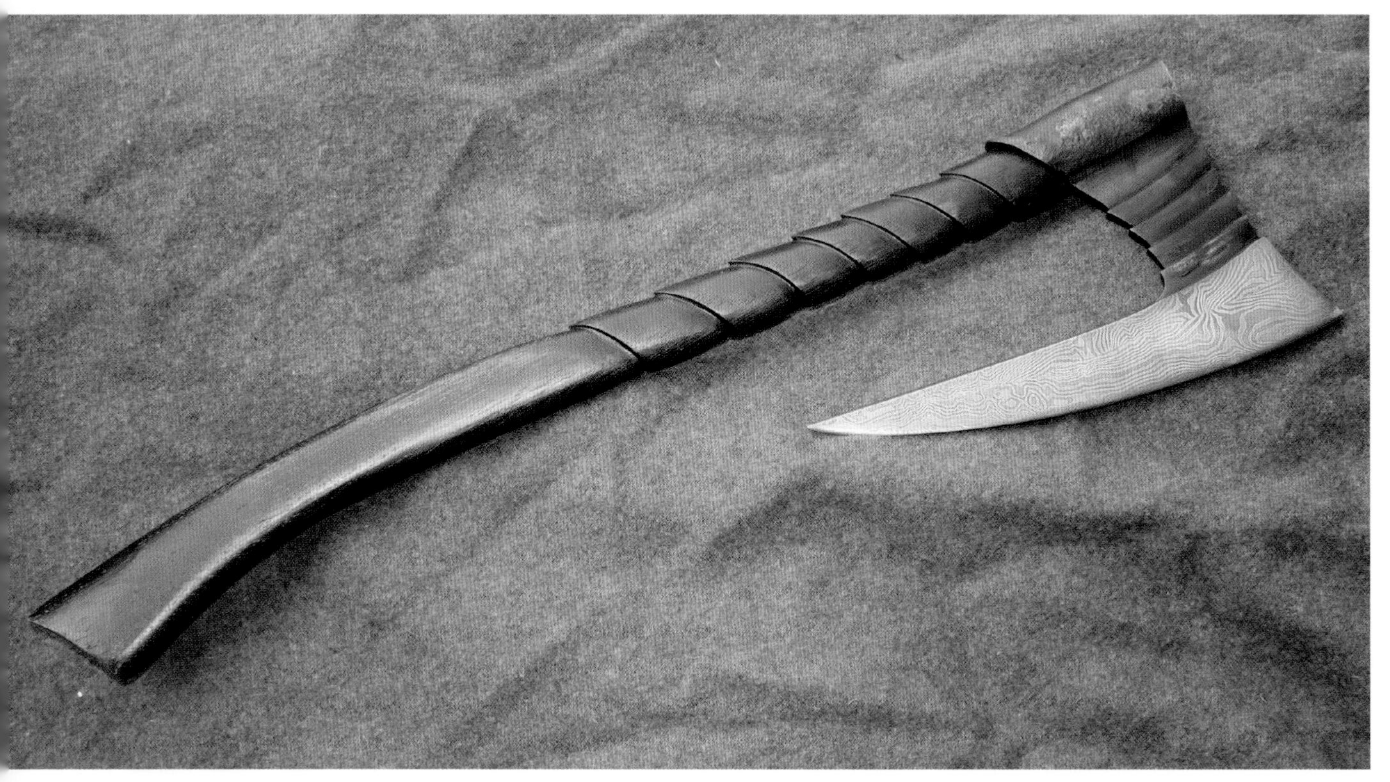

Jon Koppel

Goosewing Battle-Axe | 2007

$5^{7}/_{8}$ X $22^{7}/_{16}$ X $1^{3}/_{4}$ INCHES (15 X 57 X 4.5 CM)

Damascus steel, hickory; forged, file worked

PHOTO BY ARTIST

Mariano E. Gugliotta

Untitled | 2007

$10^5/_8$ X $1^3/_8$ INCHES (27 X 3.5 CM)

D3 steel, guayacan root; hand forged, textured

PHOTO BY ARTIST

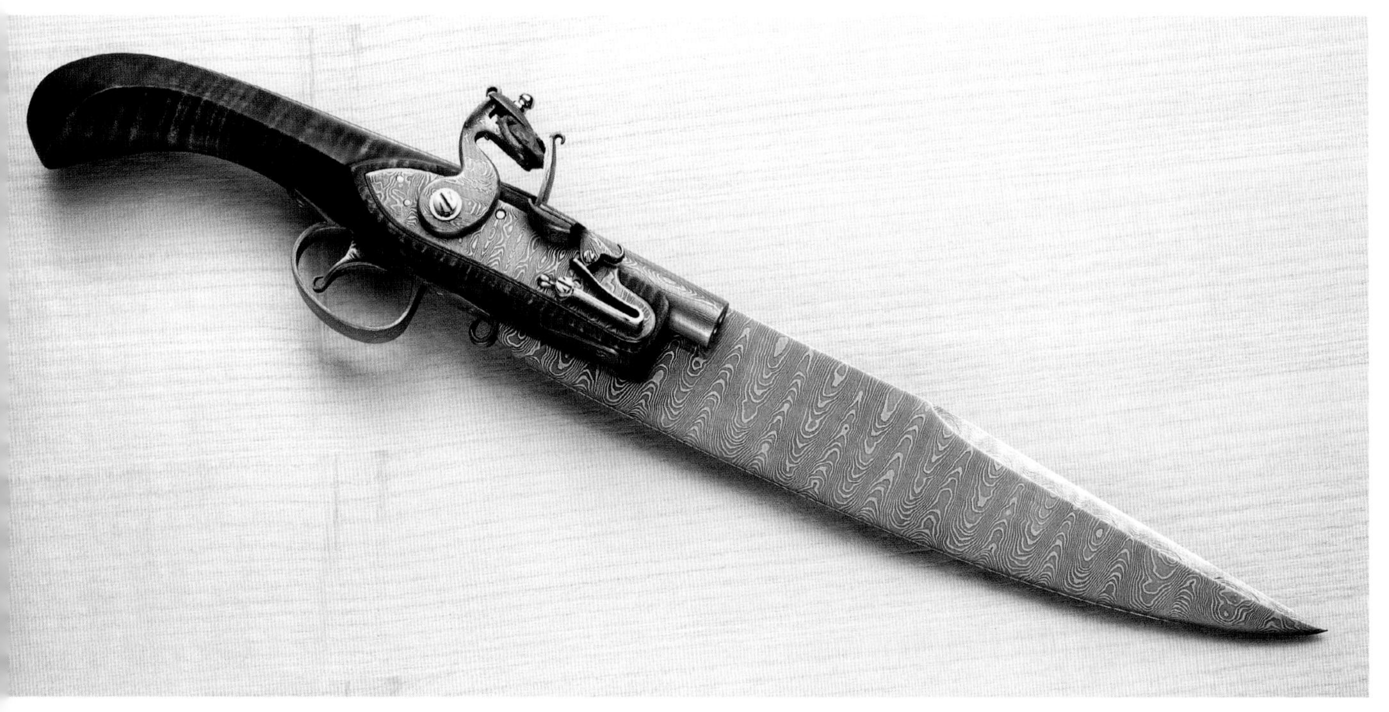

Wade Colter

Bowie Pistol | 2002

OVERALL LENGTH, 19 INCHES (48.3 CM)

Ladder-pattern Damascus steel, curly maple; forged, acid stained

PHOTO BY POINTSEVEN STUDIOS

Anders Högström

Karambit | 2007

OVERALL LENGTH, 6 5/16 INCHES (16 CM)

1050 carbon steel, bronze, leather; clay tempered, antiqued, textured

PHOTO BY JIM COOPER OF SHARPBYCOOP.COM

D'Alton Holder

40th-Anniversary Knife | 2006

OVERALL LENGTH, 8¾ INCHES (22.2 CM); BLADE, 4 INCHES (10.1 CM)

ATS-34 steel, ironwood, oosic, amber; engraved

ENGRAVED BY PAT HOLDER
PHOTO BY JIM COOPER OF SHARPBYCOOP.COM

Roger Bergh

Speed Waves

OVERALL LENGTH, 9 1/2 INCHES (24.1 CM)

Bergh mosaic Damascus steel, Damascus steel, ironwood, walrus horn, North Sea mammoth

PHOTO BY JIM COOPER OF SHARPBYCOOP.COM

Tai Goo

Topsy-Turvy Integral | 2004

1065 steel, rosewood; forged

SHEATH BY SANDY MORRISON
PHOTO BY JIM COOPER OF SHARPBYCOOP.COM

Dr. Jim Lucie

William Scagel-Style Camp Knife | 2006

OVERALL LENGTH, 14 15/16 INCHES (38 CM)

1084 steel, silver; hand forged

PHOTO BY BUDDY THOMASON

Jim Hammond

Jim Hammond 30th-Anniversary Knife | 2007

OVERALL LENGTH, 14 13/16 INCHES (37.6 CM)

440C stainless steel, India stag; hollow ground, hand rubbed

PHOTO BY JIM COOPER OF SHARPBYCOOP.COM

Steven R. Johnson

Eight-Inch Bolo—2007 Knifemaker's Guild President's Gala Knife | 2007

OVERALL LENGTH, $13\frac{3}{8}$ INCHES (34 CM)

ATS-34 steel, 416 stainless steel, Bighorn Sheep horn, sambar stag

PHOTO BY JIM COOPER OF SHARPBYCOOP.COM

J. Neilson

Mountain Thunder Bowie | 2007

OVERALL LENGTH, 21 1/4 INCHES (54 CM)

Damascus steel, stag

PHOTO BY CHUCK WARD PHOTOGRAPHY

John White

Damascus Ladder-Pattern Fighter | 2007

OVERALL LENGTH, 12¾ INCHES (32.4 CM)

Damascus steel, nickel silver, mammoth ivory, 18-karat gold; forged, grooved, file worked, fabricated

PHOTO BY CHUCK WARD PHOTOGRAPHY

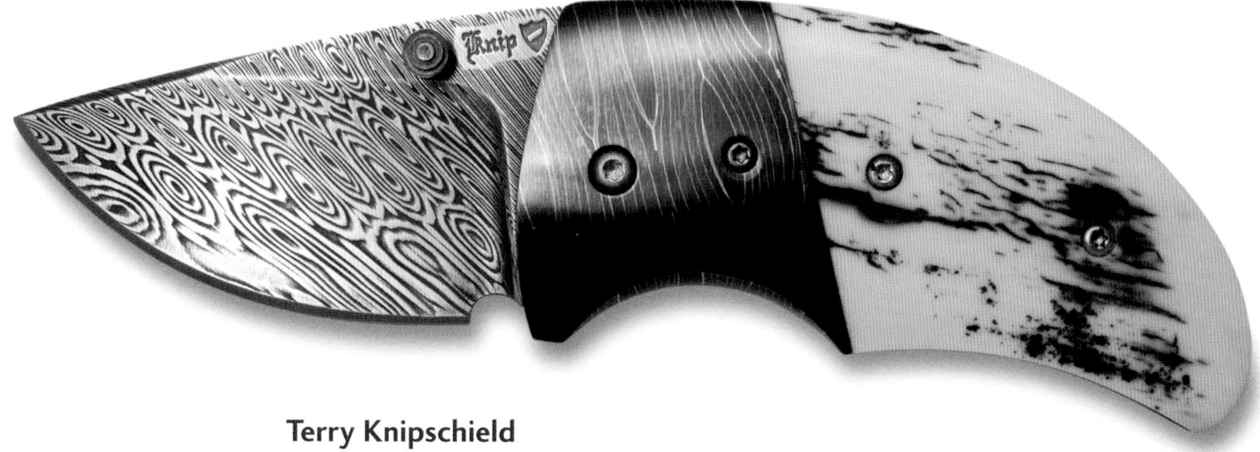

Terry Knipschield

The Little Knipper | 2007

$1\frac{3}{16}$ X $4\frac{1}{2}$ X $\frac{3}{8}$ INCHES (3 X 11.5 X 1 CM)

Damascus steel, mammoth ivory, titanium; anodized, stock removal, file worked

DAMASCUS BOLSTERS BY DELBERT EALY
PHOTO BY MATT KNIPSCHIELD

John Horrigan

End of the Trail | 2005

OVERALL LENGTH, 12 INCHES (30.5 CM)

Feather-pattern Damascus steel, buffalo horn

PHOTO BY STEVE WOODS

Joe Szilaski

Buffalo-Head Pipe Tomahawk | 2006

HEAD, 8 INCHES (20.3 CM)

W-2 tool steel, silver, bird's-eye maple; forged, carved, inlaid, engraved

PHOTO BY LORI SZILASKI

Aad van Rijswijk

The Eagle | 2002

OVERALL LENGTH, $6^1/_2$ INCHES (16.5 CM)

Stainless rose-pattern Damascus steel, mammoth ivory, 24-karat white gold, 24-karat yellow gold, 24-karat pink gold; engraved, inlaid

PHOTO BY BOB VAN TIENHOVEN

Harvey Dean

Duelist Folding Bowie | 2005

OVERALL LENGTH, 12 INCHES (30.5 CM)

Ladder-pattern Damascus steel, mother-of-pearl; forged, inlaid

PHOTO BY STEVE WOODS

Leon Treiber

The Texas Ranger Mammoth | 2007

OVERALL LENGTH, 8 3/8 INCHES (21.3 CM)

416 stainless steel, sterling silver, mammoth ivory; inlaid, engraved, file worked

ENGRAVED BY A.E. SCOTT
PHOTOS BY ARTIST

Donald J. Vogt

Emerald Dagger | 2004

10 1/8 X 1 1/8 X 7/16 INCHES (25.7 X 2.9 X 1.1 CM)

Damascus steel, 440C stainless steel, 14-karat gold, emeralds, abalone, titanium; ground, carved, heat-treated, shaped, embellished, mounted, inlaid, engraved, profiled, hardened, hammered, file worked, color anodized

PHOTO BY POINTSEVEN STUDIOS

Warren Osborne

Model 28 | 2006

OVERALL LENGTH, 7 1/8 INCHES (18.1 CM)

CPM-154 stainless steel, 416 stainless steel, jasper, gold; inlaid

PHOTO BY JIM COOPER OF SHARPBYCOOP.COM

Dusty Moulton

Raptor | 2004

OVERALL LENGTH, 11 3/4 INCHES (29.8 CM)

Damascus steel, mammoth ivory; engraved

DAMASCUS STEEL BY JIM FERGUSON
PHOTO BY JIM COOPER OF SHARPBYCOOP.COM

Jody Muller

Monster Serrations | 2008

OVERALL LENGTH, 11 INCHES (28 CM)

Damascus steel, mammoth ivory, titanium

PHOTO BY JIM COOPER OF SHARPBYCOOP.COM

Don Hanson III

Monster Slip Joint | 2007

OVERALL LENGTH, 8¾ INCHES (22.2 CM)

Hanson ladder-pattern Damascus steel, amber stag bone

PHOTO BY JIM COOPER OF SHARPBYCOOP.COM

Johnny Stout

The Accolade | 2007

OVERALL LENGTH, 5⅞ INCHES (14.9 CM)

Vines-and-roses Damascus steel, mosaic Damascus steel, India sambar stag; engraved

DAMASCUS STEEL BY DEVIN THOMAS
ENGRAVED BY JOE MASON
PHOTO BY JIM COOPER OF SHARPBYCOOP.COM

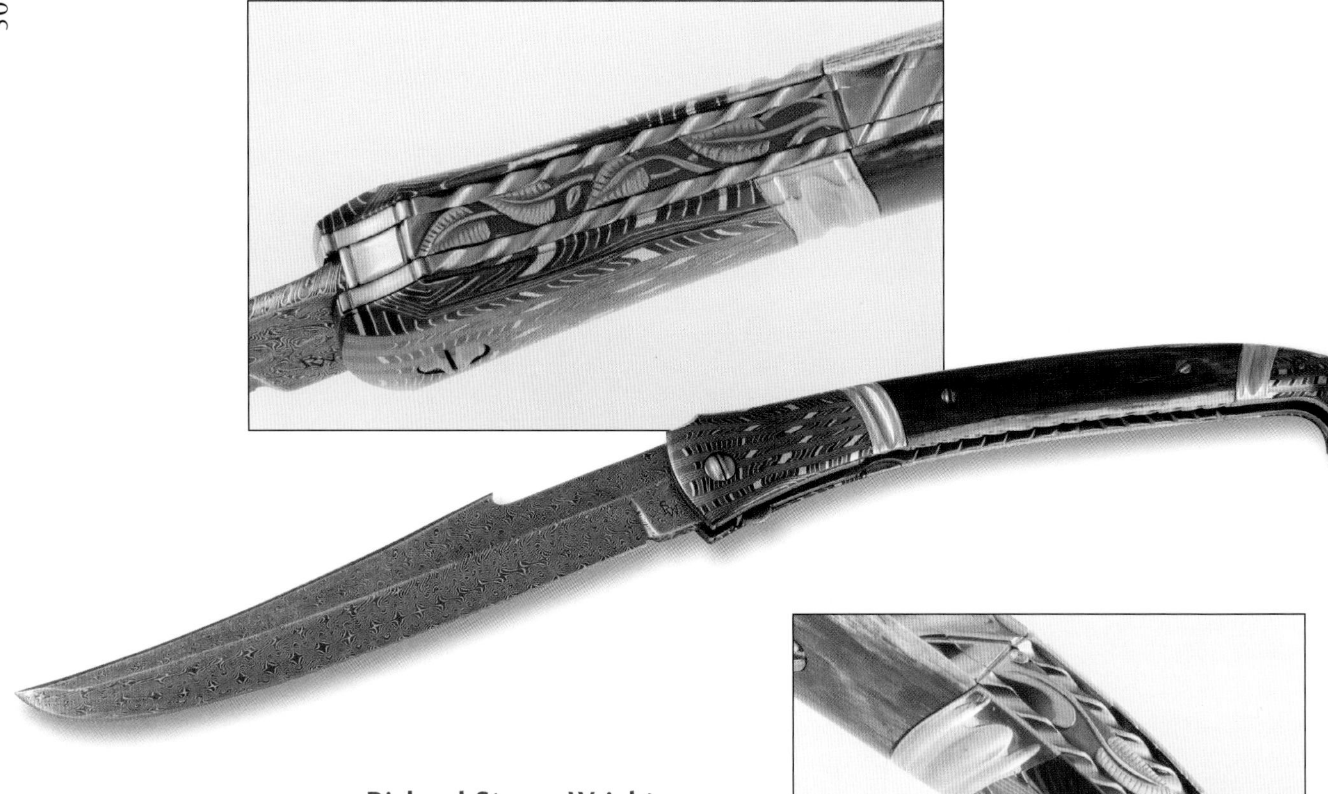

Richard Steven Wright

Ambidextrous Bolster-Release Persian-Dagger Switchblade | 2007

OVERALL LENGTH, 12 9/16 INCHES (31.9 CM); BLADE, 5 5/16 INCHES (15.1 CM)

Turkish-twist Damascus steel, mosaic Damascus steel, German silver, mammoth ivory, titanium, elephant ivory; forged, ground, carved

TURKISH-TWIST DAMASCUS STEEL BY JERRY RADOS
MOSAIC DAMASCUS STEEL BY ROBERT EGGERLING
PHOTOS BY ARTIST

William Henry Studio

B3 Spryte | 2003–2006

OVERALL LENGTH, 4⅝ INCHES (11.7 CM)

Ribbon-lace Damascus steel, leather, beads

PHOTO BY JIM COOPER OF SHARPBYCOOP.COM

Howard Hitchmough

Deco Sunshine | 2007

OVERALL LENGTH, 6 1/16 INCHES (15.5 CM)

Stainless Damascus steel, stainless steel, titanium, 18-karat gold; engraved, inlaid

ENGRAVED AND INLAID BY TIM GEORGE
PHOTO BY POINTSEVEN STUDIOS

Van Barnett

Folding Knife: Raven | 2003

OVERALL LENGTH, 7 7/16 INCHES (19 CM)

Ladder-pattern Damascus steel, 14-karat yellow gold, 24-karat gold, steel, emeralds, diamonds, sapphires, titanium; forged, etched, carved, textured, engraved, inlaid, file worked

PHOTO BY POINTSEVEN STUDIOS

Juergen Steinau

Knife-Objekt 970923.1 | 1997

8½ X 1¼ X ½ INCHES (21.6 X 3.2 X 1.3 CM)

440B stainless steel, pure nickel, black pearl

PHOTO BY POINTSEVEN STUDIOS

T.R. Overeynder

Model 17 | 2006

OVERALL LENGTH, 7 3/16 INCHES (18.3 CM)

Hornet's-nest Damascus steel, black-lip pearl, 24-karat gold; engraved, inlaid

BLADE STEEL BY MIKE NORRIS
ENGRAVED AND INLAID BY JOE MASON
PHOTO BY POINTSEVEN STUDIOS

Rick Dunkerley

Untitled | 2007

Mosaic Damascus steel, 1084 steel, 18-karat gold, 24-karat gold, diamond; nitre blued, filed, inlaid

PHOTO BY ARTIST

Don Hanson III

Abalone Gent's Folder | 2004

OVERALL LENGTH, 6 1/2 INCHES (16.5 CM)

Mosaic Damascus steel, green abalone, 18-karat rose gold, bail, twisted wire, titanium; forged, inlaid, file worked

PHOTO BY JIM COOPER OF SHARPBYCOOP.COM

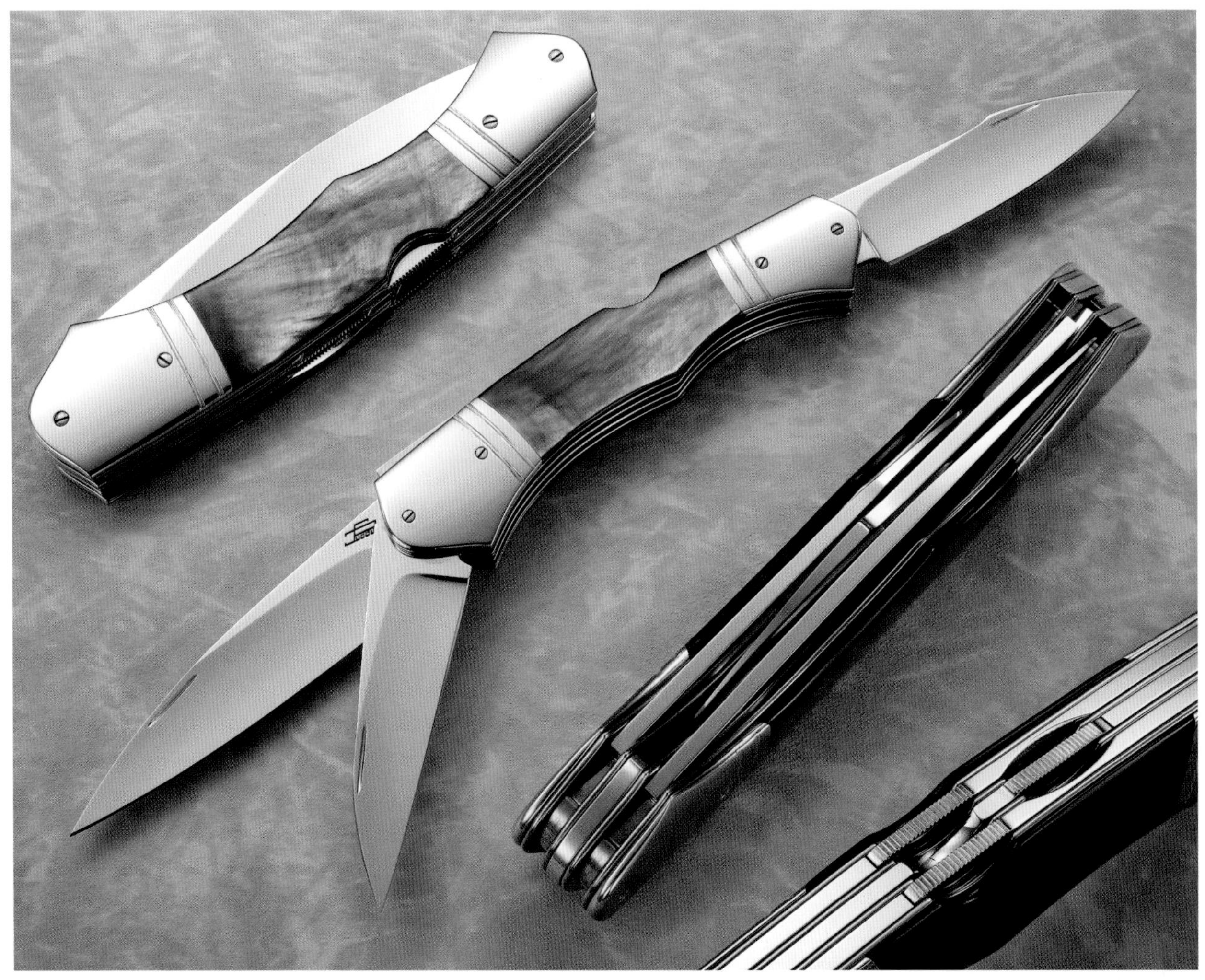

Salvatore Puddu

Tree Blade Lock-Back Folder | 2002–2004

OVERALL LENGTH, 6 7/8 INCHES (17.5 CM)

ATS-34 steel, 416 stainless steel, mother-of-pearl, 24-karat gold, titanium, 18-karat gold; inlaid

PHOTO BY JIM COOPER OF SHARPBYCOOP.COM

Kaj Embretsen

Inter-Frame Back-Lock Fighter

Explosion Damascus steel, black-lip pearl, gold; inlaid

PHOTO BY JIM COOPER OF SHARPBYCOOP.COM

Owen Wood

Art Nouveau Folding Knife | 1995

OVERALL LENGTH, 6 INCHES (15.2 CM)

Composite Damascus steel, titanium, 303 stainless steel, gold; inlaid, blued

INLAID BY ARMIN WINKLER
PHOTO BY JIM COOPER OF SHARPBYCOOP.COM

Lloyd Hale

Rip Tide | 2005

440C stainless steel, abalone

PHOTO BY JIM COOPER OF SHARPBYCOOP.COM

Gail Lunn

Carmel Creme | 2007

OVERALL LENGTH, 8 15/16 INCHES (22.8 CM)

Mosaic Damascus steel, mother-of-pearl; file worked, fluted

PHOTO BY JIM COOPER OF SHARPBYCOOP.COM

Ken Steigerwalt

Untitled | 2004

BLADE, 3 1/4 INCHES (8.3 CM)

Stainless Damascus steel, titanium; carved, integral constructed

DAMASCUS STEEL BY DEVIN THOMAS
PHOTO BY JIM COOPER OF SHARPBYCOOP.COM

Wolfgang Loerchner

Persian-Style Folding Knife | 2007

OVERALL LENGTH, 8 INCHES (20.3 CM)

440C stainless steel, 416 stainless steel, Damascus steel, gold, black-lip mother-of-pearl; carved, inlaid

PHOTO BY JIM COOPER OF SHARPBYCOOP.COM

Ken Steigerwalt

Untitled | 2006

BLADE, 3 1/2 INCHES (8.8 CM)

Damascus steel, black pearl, 18-karat gold; carved, inlaid

DAMASCUS STEEL BY DEVIN THOMAS
PHOTO BY JIM COOPER OF SHARPBYCOOP.COM

Matthew Lerch

Paia Dagger | 2008

OVERALL LENGTH, 8 1/2 INCHES (21.2 CM)

Damascus steel, double stainless steel, titanium; inlaid, filed

STEEL AND INLAY BY MIKE NORRIS
FILED BY MARY JO LERCH
PHOTO BY JIM COOPER OF SHARPBYCOOP.COM

Des Horn

Folding Knife: Model HBP-02 | 2006

OVERALL LENGTH, 6 9/16 INCHES (16.7 CM); BLADE, 3 INCHES (7.4 CM)

Stainless Damascus steel, 416 stainless steel; double tempered, cryogenically treated, hand carved, threaded

PHOTO BY MIKE FELLOWS

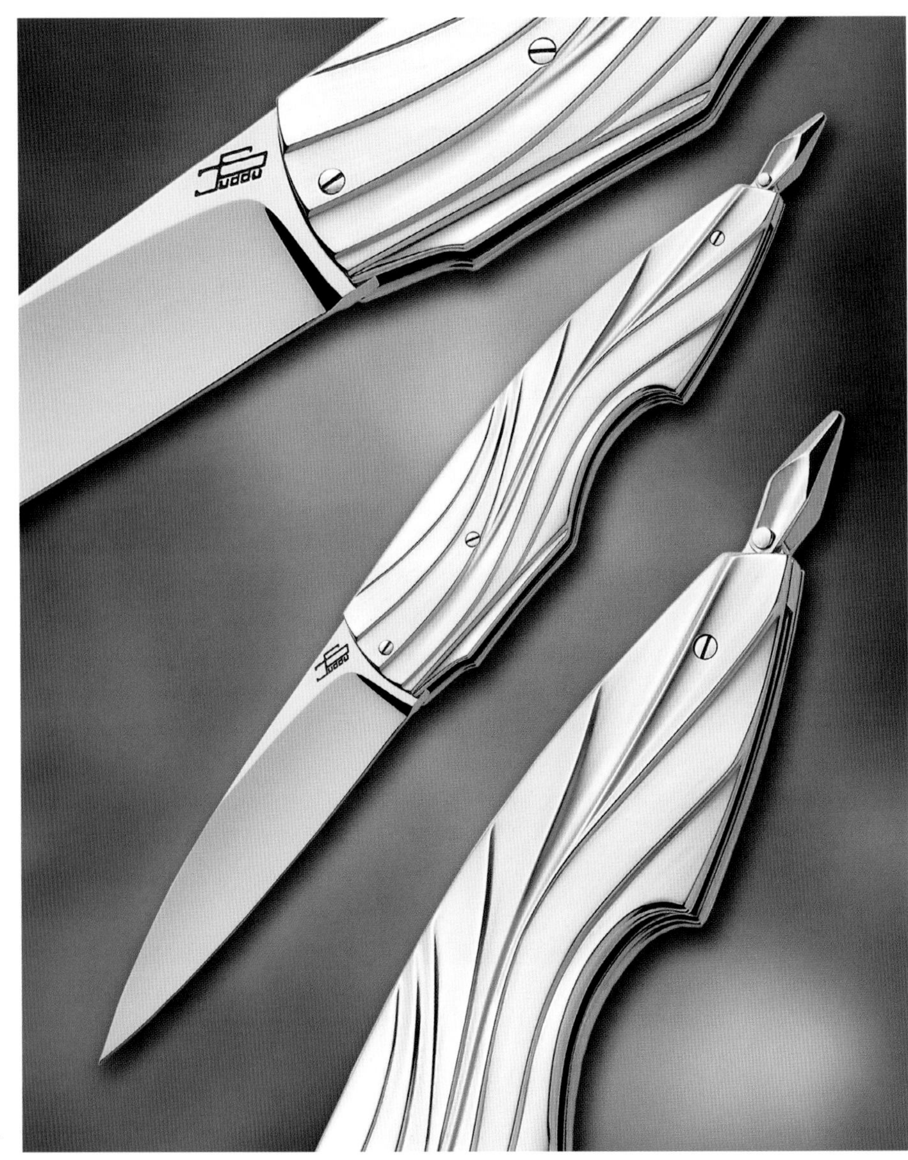

Salvatore Puddu

Queen | 2005

OVERALL LENGTH, 6 9/16 INCHES (16.7 CM)

Stainless steel; sculpted

PHOTO BY FRANCESCO PACHÍ

Tim Herman
Wolfgang Loerchner

Cosmic Tanto | 1991

OVERALL LENGTH, 7 3/4 INCHES (19.6 CM)

Raindrop pattern Damascus steel, 416 stainless steel; stock removal, carved

CARVED BY WOLFGANG LOERCHNER
PHOTO BY JIM COOPER OF SHARPBYCOOP.COM

Jeff Claiborne

Two-Blade Doctor's Knife | 2007

3 1/8 X 1/2 X 3/8 INCHES (7.9 X 1.3 X 1 CM)

52100 steel, 416 stainless steel, brown bone; forged, ground, hand rubbed, integral milled

PHOTO BY TERRILL HOFFMAN

Steve W. Hoel

Large Coke Bottle with Black Jade | 1995

BLADE, $3\frac{3}{8}$ INCHES (8.6 CM)

ATS-34 stainless steel, 416 stainless steel, black jade; heat-treated, inlaid

PHOTO BY JIM COOPER OF SHARPBYCOOP.COM

Emmanuel Esposito

Rhino | 2007

OVERALL LENGTH, 8 INCHES (20.4 CM)

RWL-34 steel, green canvas Micarta, stainless steel

PHOTO BY FRANCESCO PACHÍ

Marcin Bona

Lizard | 2006

7/8 X 6 1/2 X 1/8 INCHES (2.3 X 16.5 X 0.3 CM)

D2 steel, green canvas Micarta, brass; hollow ground, satin finished

PHOTO BY JIM COOPER OF SHARPBYCOOP.COM

Christoph Deringer

Chef's Knife | 2006

OVERALL LENGTH, 14 INCHES (35.5 CM)

01 steel, California walnut, nickel silver, copper; hand forged, heat-treated

PHOTO BY JIM COOPER OF SHARPBYCOOP.COM

Schuyler Lovestrand

Model H-10 Drop-Point Hunter | 1985

OVERALL LENGTH, $8\frac{5}{8}$ INCHES (22 CM)

ATS-34, Brazilian rosewood

PHOTO BY JIM COOPER OF SHARPBYCOOP.COM

Don Hanson III

Sinistre | 2007

OVERALL LENGTH, 12½ INCHES (31.8 CM)

Hanson W-2 tool steel, Hanson Damascus steel, vivid hamon, antique ivory, 18-karat gold pins; forged

PHOTO BY JIM COOPER OF SHARPBYCOOP.COM

Bob Kramer

Untitled | 2007

$2\frac{3}{8}$ X 13 X 1 INCHES (6 X 33 X 2.5 CM)

Flip-flop Damascus steel, brass, ironwood

PHOTO BY JEFF CRAWFORD

Bob Kramer

Untitled | 2007

1 15/16 X 15 5/16 X 1 INCHES
(5 X 39 X 2.5 CM)

Mosaic Damascus steel, mokume gane, thuya burl, blackwood

PHOTO BY JEFF CRAWFORD

Shosui Takeda

Ken-Nata Hunter | 2007

OVERALL LENGTH, 15 15/16 INCHES (40.5 CM)

Aogami Super Steel, oak; wound, lacquered, hand forged

PHOTO BY HIDETOSHI FUKUBA

Thomas Haslinger

New Generation Chef's Knives | 2006

LONGEST, 15 5/16 INCHES (39 CM)

CPM S30V stainless steel, blue G10 steel, silver twill G10 steel; stroke finished, overlaid

PHOTO BY JIM COOPER OF SHARPBYCOOP.COM

Bob Kramer

Untitled | 2007

$2\frac{3}{8}$ X $15\frac{5}{16}$ X 1 INCHES (6 X 39 X 2.5 CM)

52100 steel, ironwood, brass

PHOTO BY JEFF CRAWFORD

Jerry L. Fisk

Bandolero Southwest Bowie | 2008

OVERALL LENGTH, 9 INCHES (22.9 CM)

Damascus steel, ivory, stainless steel, beads, fossil walrus; framed, engraved

PHOTO BY CHUCK WARD

Laurent Doussot

Untitled | 2006

OVERALL LENGTH, 12 13/16 INCHES (32.5 CM)

ATS-34 steel, bronze, reindeer horn; cast

PHOTO BY CONTRE JOUR STUDIO

Jot Singh Khalsa

Sculpted Folding Knife | 2004

OVERALL LENGTH, 8 INCHES (20.3 CM)

Braided nickel Damascus steel, mokume gane, paua shells; carved, inlaid

PHOTO BY JIM COOPER OF SHARPBYCOOP.COM

Anders Högström

Stiletto | 2006

OVERALL LENGTH, 17 11/16 INCHES (45 CM)

Högström Damascus steel, copper, mammoth tooth, leather; antiqued, textured

PHOTO BY JIM COOPER OF SHARPBYCOOP.COM

André Thorburn

Untitled: Model No. L18 | 2004

OVERALL LENGTH, 6¼ INCHES (15.9 CM)

High-carbon Damascus steel, mammoth ivory; hot-gun blued, etched, buffed

DAMASCUS STEEL BY ETTORÉ GIANFERRARI
PHOTO BY JIM COOPER OF SHARPBYCOOP.COM

John Davis

JD Explosion | 2006

OVERALL LENGTH, 7 INCHES (17.8 CM)

Damascus steel, mammoth ivory

PHOTO BY JIM COOPER OF SHARPBYCOOP.COM

Philip Booth

Untitled | 2004

OVERALL LENGTH, 6 1/8 INCHES (90 CM)

Persian Damascus steel, checkerboard-pattern Damascus steel, 01 steel, ivory; file worked, blued

PHOTO BY JIM COOPER OF SHARPBYCOOP.COM

Jeremy Krammes

Dragon Folder | 2007

OVERALL LENGTH, $7^{1}/_{16}$ INCHES (18 CM)

Fireclone stainless Damascus steel, dragon-skin Damascus steel, titanium; hand carved, anodized, file worked

FIRECLONE DAMASCUS STEEL BY MIKE NORRIS
DRAGON-SKIN DAMASCUS STEEL BY BERTIE RIETVELD
PHOTO BY JIM COOPER OF SHARPBYCOOP.COM

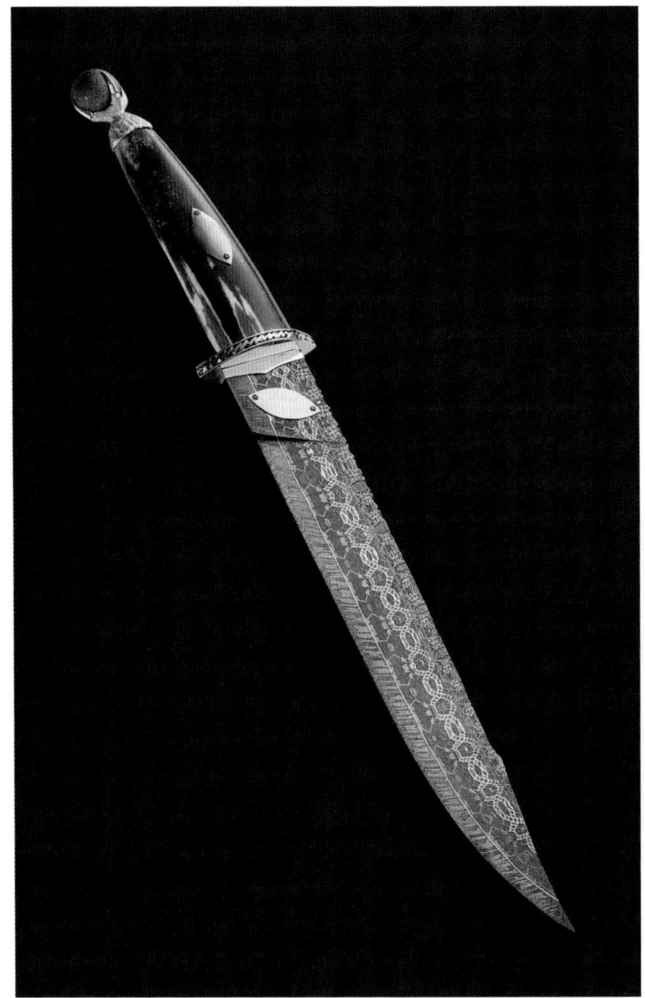

Johan Gustafsson

Stallions | 2004

OVERALL LENGTH, $7^{7}/_{16}$ INCHES (19 CM)

Mosaic Damascus steel, walrus ivory, gold-plated screws; forge welded, drilled, heat-treated, polished

PHOTO BY JIM COOPER OF SHARPBYCOOP.COM

Antonio Fogarizzu

Damascus Folder | 2006

OVERALL LENGTH, $7^{1}/_{16}$ (18 CM)

Mosaic Damascus steel, titanium

PHOTO BY JIM COOPER OF SHARPBYCOOP.COM

Don Lozier

Casino Royale Boot Dagger | 2007

OVERALL LENGTH, $8\frac{7}{8}$ INCHES (22.5 CM)

Stainless raindrop-pattern Damascus steel; hot blued, cold rolled

DAMASCUS STEEL BY MIKE NORRIS
PHOTO BY JIM COOPER OF SHARPBYCOOP.COM

Jens Ansø

Outbreak Flipper | 2008

OVERALL LENGTH, 8 2/5 INCHES (21 CM)

RWL-34 steel, titanium; textured

PHOTO BY JIM COOPER OF SHARPBYCOOP.COM

Reinhard Tschager

Pocket Dagger with Symmetrical Blade | 2007

OVERALL LENGTH, 4 15/16 INCHES (12.6 CM)

Tortoiseshell, 18-karat gold; engraved

PHOTO BY FRANCESCO PACHÍ

Dave Larsen

Danny's Skinning Axe | 2006

OVERALL LENGTH, 16 INCHES (40.6 CM)

01 steel, paper phenolic, mosaic pins; file worked, carved

PHOTO BY JIM COOPER OF SHARPBYCOOP.COM

³/8 INCHES (27 CM)

us steel, mammoth ivory, gold, copper;

d, hand engraved

OPER OF SHARPBYCOOP.COM

Yuan-Fan Chen

Willow Leaf Knife | 2007

37 3/8 X 3 1/8 X 2 3/8 INCHES (95 X 8 X 6 CM)

D2 steel, ebony, cotton rope, calfskin, nickel alloy; carved, ground, polished

PHOTO BY ARTIST

Steve E. Hill

Cactus Jack | 2005

OVERALL LENGTH, 14 15/16 INCHES (38 CM)

Twist Damascus steel, mammoth ivory, titanium; sculpted, pierced, heat and anodized colored, file worked, carved

PHOTO BY JIM COOPER OF SHARPBYCOOP.COM

Keith Ouye

Longevity | 2008

OVERALL LENGTH, $9\,^{1}/_{8}$ INCHES (23.2 CM)

S30V stainless steel, 6AL4V titanium; engraved, heat-treated

ENGRAVED BY C.J. CAI
HEAT-TREATED BY PAUL BOS
PHOTO BY JIM COOPER OF SHARPBYCOOP.COM

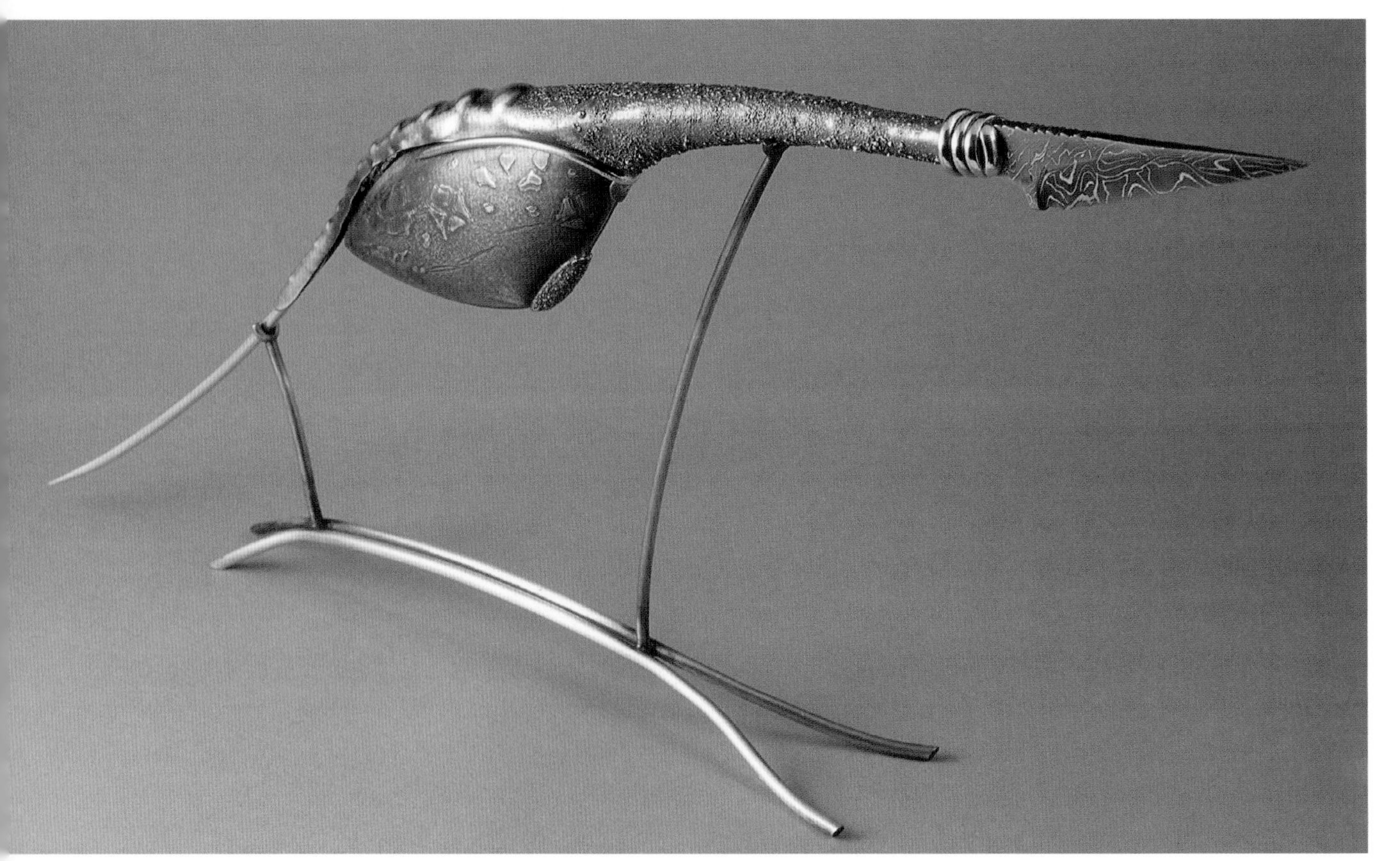

Chantal Gilbert

L'Oie Blanche | 2001

OVERALL LENGTH, 14 9/16 INCHES (37 CM)

Damascus steel, silver

PHOTO BY YUAN BINET

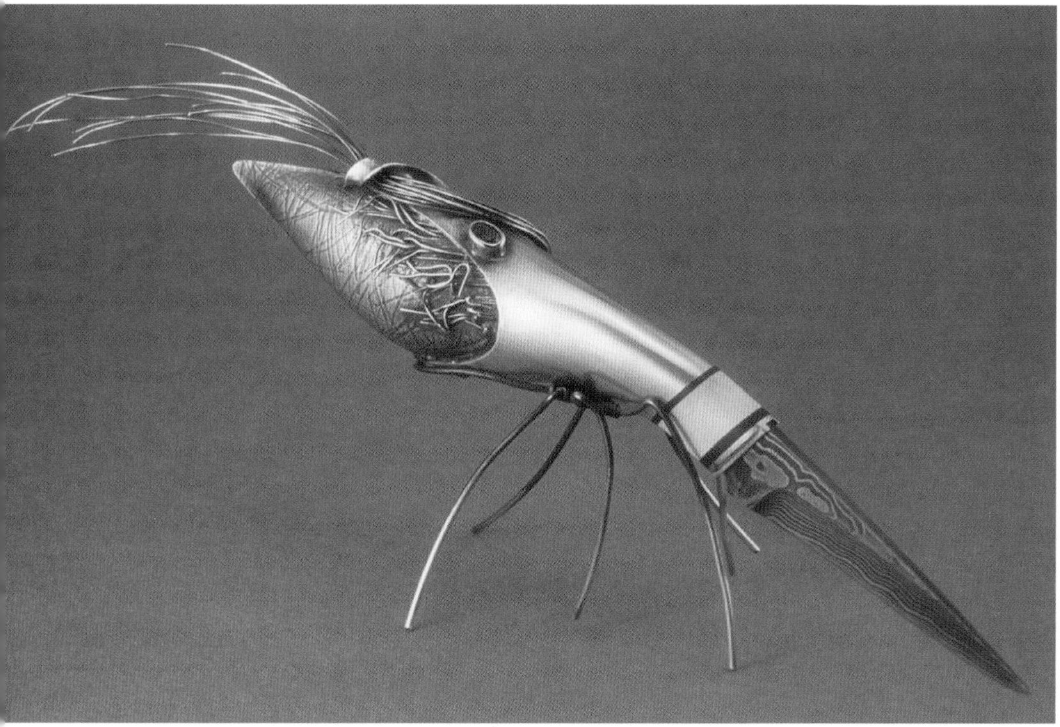

Chantal Gilbert

Mademoiselle | 2001

OVERALL LENGTH, $10\frac{1}{4}$ INCHES (26 CM)

Damascus steel, silver, 18-karat gold, mammoth ivory, rhodolite

PHOTO BY YUAN BINET

Chantal Gilbert

La Caresse | 2004

OVERALL LENGTH, $11\frac{13}{16}$ INCHES (30 CM)

Damascus steel, sterling silver, bronze

PHOTO BY YUAN BINET

Owen Mapp

Thor's Gift to Odin | 2000

16 1/8 X 1 9/16 X 1 3/16 INCHES (41 X 4 X 3 CM)

Damascus steel, elephant ivory, garnets, sterling silver, brass

PHOTO BY HANNE ERIKSEN

Harumi Hirayama

Maelstrom Series Rear-Lock Folder: Male and Female Carp | 2008

MALE (LARGER), 8 1/16 X 1 5/16 X 3/4 INCHES (20.5 X 3.3 X 2 CM);
FEMALE (SMALLER), 6 7/8 X 1 1/16 X 3/4 INCHES (17.5 X 2.8 X 2 CM)

440C stainless steel, silver, 18-karat gold, ironwood, mother-of-pearl, apple coral; carved, inlaid

COLLECTION OF DAVID COHEN
PHOTOS BY TOMO HASEGAWA

Larry Lunn

Eye of the Tiger | 2007

OVERALL LENGTH, 27 11/16 INCHES (70.3 CM)

San Mei nickel Damascus steel, mosaic Damascus steel, elephant ivory; scrimshawed

SCRIMSHAWED BY FAUSTINA
PHOTO BY JIM COOPER OF SHARPBYCOOP.COM

Norman E. Sandow

Model 8 | 2005

6 X 1/2 X 8 INCHES (17 X 1.2 X 20 CM)

ATS-34 steel, mother-of-pearl, titanium, mammoth ivory; scrimshawed

SCRIMSHAWED BY MICHELLE CLAIRE
PHOTO BY ARTIST

Stephen Mackrill, Jr.

Death of the Dinosaur | 2006

$8^{3}/_{16}$ X 10 X $^{3}/_{16}$ INCHES (20.8 X 25.4 X 0.4 CM)

Damascus steel, hippopotamus tooth, buffalo horn; scrimshawed

DAMASCUS STEEL BY DEVLIN THOMAS
SCRIMSHAWED BY BRUCE VAN BLERK
PHOTO BY POINTSEVEN STUDIOS

Charles Maurice Roulin

Mammouth | 2005

OVERALL LENGTH, 8 5/8 INCHES (22 CM)

440C stainless steel, mammoth ivory

PHOTOS BY ARTIST

Mike Skellern

Wolfhound—Aikuchi | 2005

8 1/8 X 15/16 INCHES (20.6 X 2.4 CM)

Stainless Damascus steel, titanium, mammoth ivory; scrimshawed

SCRIMSHAWED BY TOI SKELLERN
PHOTO BY ARTIST

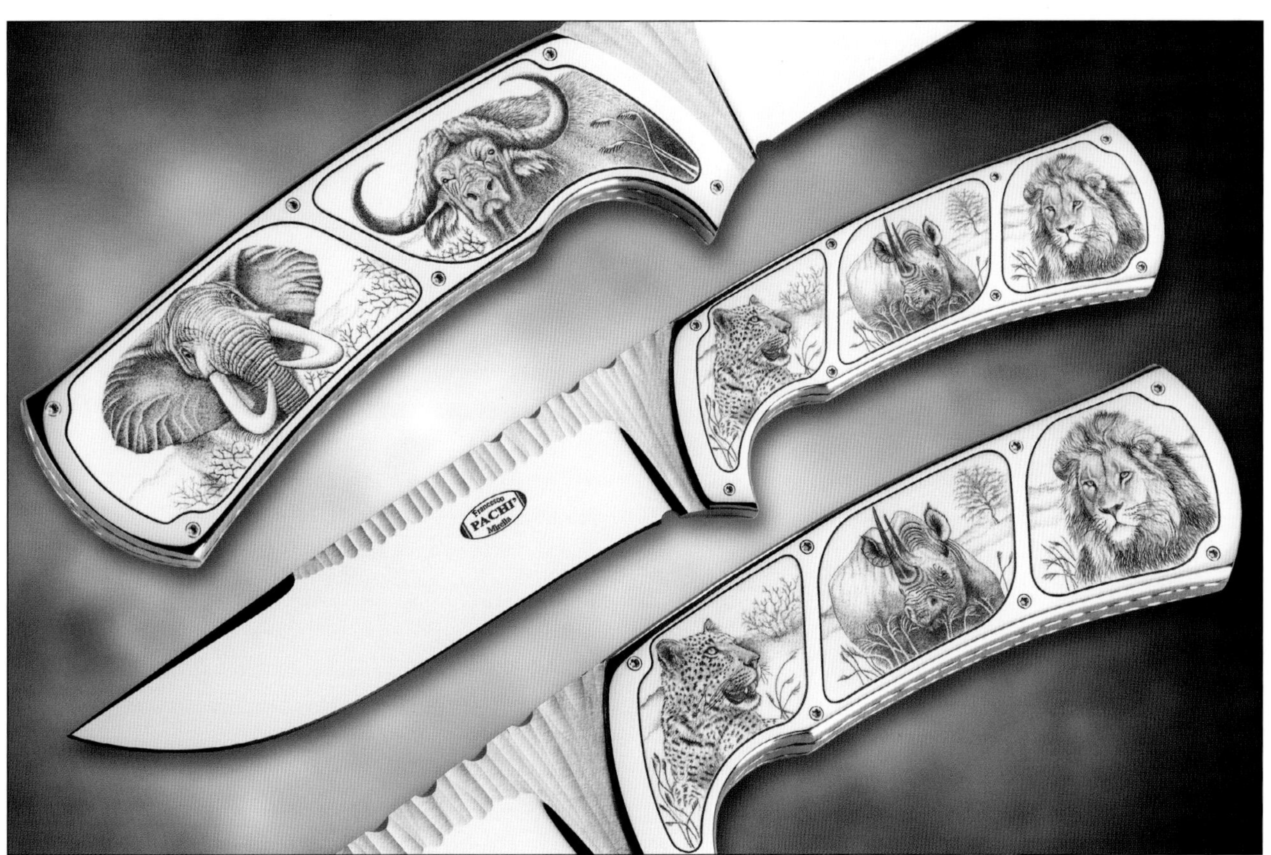

Francesco Pachí
Mirella Pachí

African Big Five | 2004

OVERALL LENGTH, 10$\frac{7}{16}$ INCHES (26.5 CM)

RWL-34 steel, white mammoth ivory; scrimshawed

PHOTO BY ARTIST

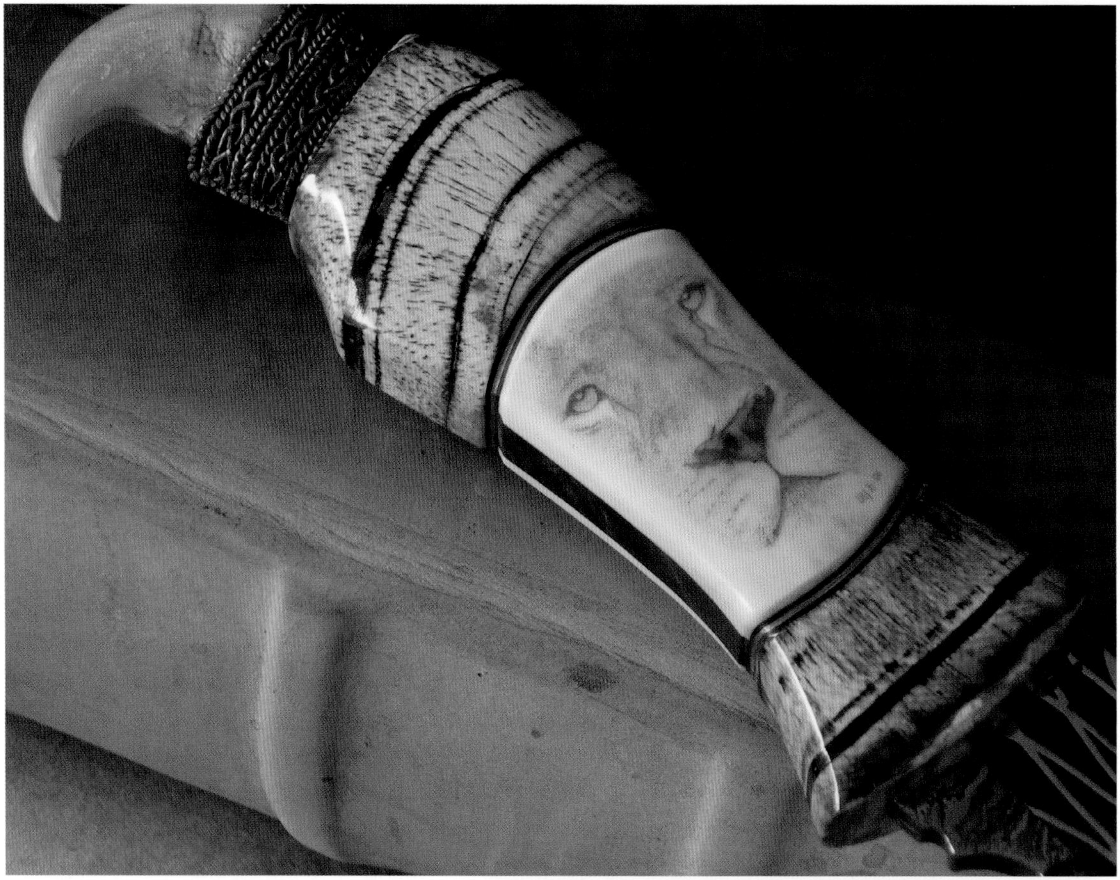

Carl Michael Almquist

The Shadow of a Lion | 2006

7 7/8 X 1 1/4 X 11/16 INCHES (20 X 3.2 X 1.8 CM)

Mammoth ivory, lion claw; scrimshawed

PHOTOS BY ARTIST

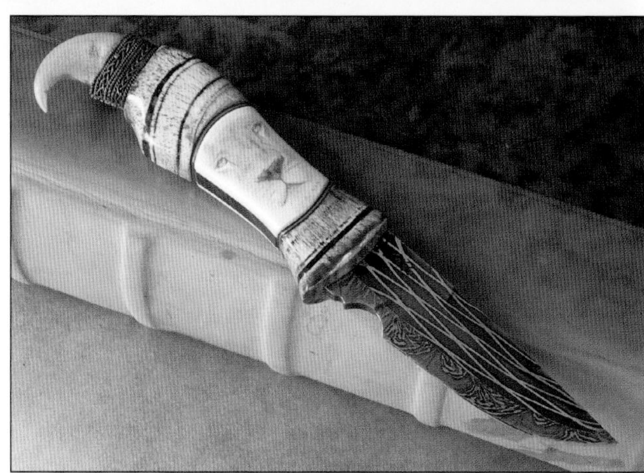

Jot Singh Khalsa

Gentleman's Folding Knife | 1997

OVERALL LENGTH, 8¾ INCHES (22.2 CM)

Damascus steel, natural jasper, 24-karat gold, stainless steel, mother-of-pearl; engraved, inlaid

ENGRAVED AND INLAID BY CHRIS MEYER
PHOTO BY POINTSEVEN STUDIOS

Chantal Gilbert

Obseléte | 2002

OVERALL LENGTH, $10^{5}/_{8}$ INCHES (27 CM)

Silver, bronze, fossil mammoth ivory, ebony, feather

PHOTO BY YUAN BINET

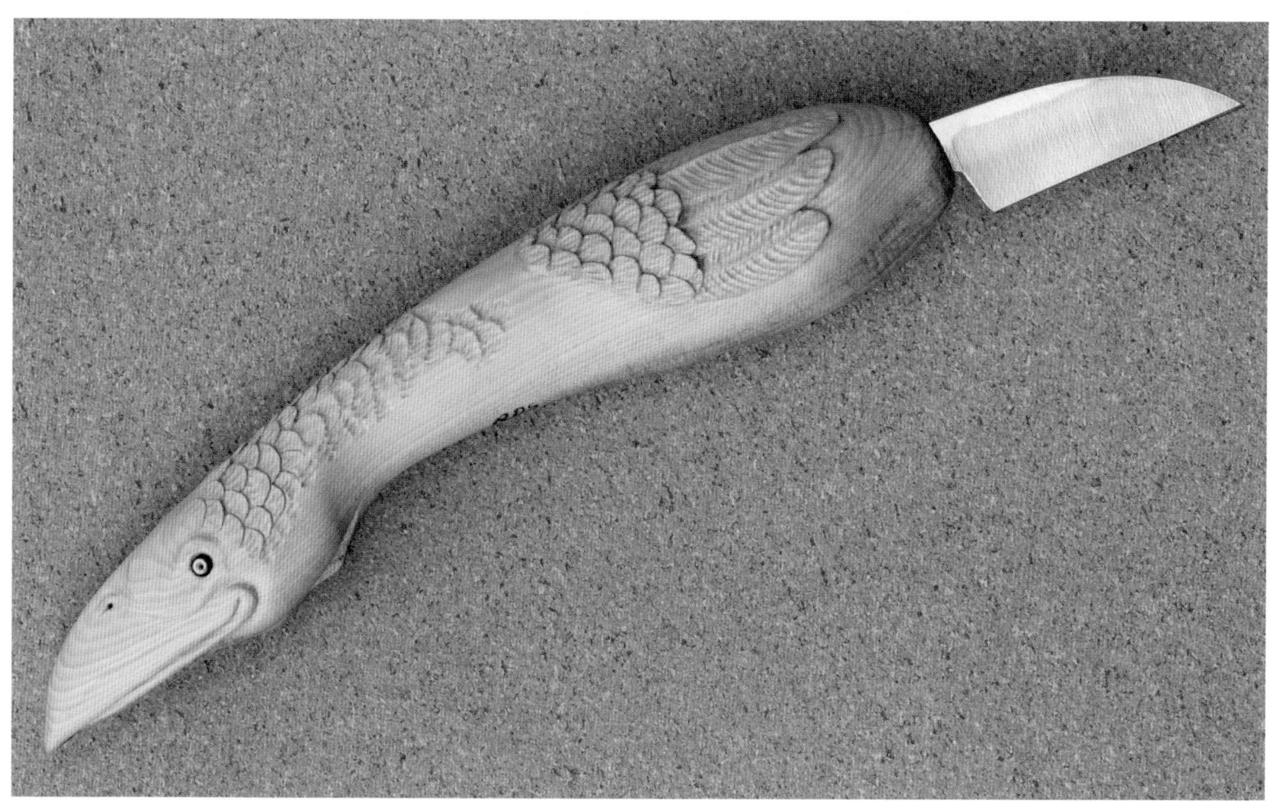

Robert Dane Shaw

Wood Carving Knife with Bird Form Handle | 2007

OVERALL LENGTH, 9 13/16 INCHES (25 CM)

440C stainless steel, cedar, glass bead; carved, textured, finished

PHOTO BY ARTIST

Fabrizio Silvestrelli

Lauro Dagger | 2007

OVERALL LENGTH, 7 7/16 INCHES (19 CM)

Inox Damascus steel, tiger coral

PHOTO BY FRANCESCO PACHÍ

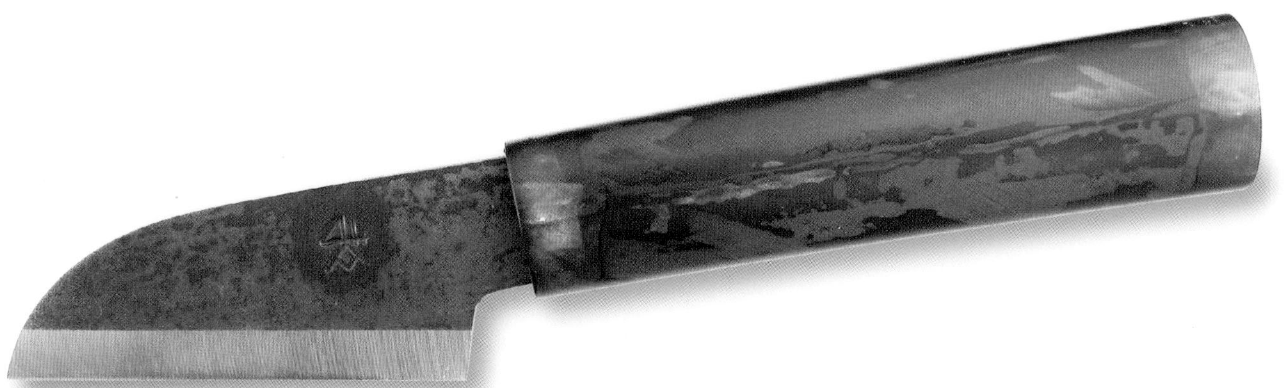

Antoine Van Loocke

Ultimate Mtm | 2007

$1\frac{9}{16}$ X $7\frac{7}{8}$ X $\frac{3}{4}$ INCHES (4 X 20 X 2 CM)

High-speed steel-carbon composite

PHOTO BY ARTIST

Thomas Haslinger

Conquistador | 2007

19¼ X 7$^{11}/_{16}$ X ¼ INCHES (49 X 19.5 X 0.6 CM)

Damascus steel, stainless Damascus steel, bronze, 14-karat gold, mammoth ivory, garnets; forged, carved, textured, soldered

DAMASCUS STEEL BY MIKE NORRIS
PHOTO BY ARTIST

Yuan-Fan Chen

Moon-Like Bend Knife | 2007

27 1/8 X 2 3/4 X 1 15/16 INCHES (69 X 7 X 5 CM)

D2 steel, ivory, African ironwood, ebony, calfskin, sharkskin; carved, ground, hand polished, dyed, hand sewn

PHOTO BY ARTIST

Daniel Winkler

Frontier Bowie and Hunter Set | 2003

BOWIE (LEFT), OVERALL LENGTH, 12½ INCHES (31.8 CM);
HUNTER (RIGHT), OVERALL LENGTH, 7½ INCHES (19.1 CM)

Ladder-pattern Damascus steel, steel, elk antler, nickel silver

PHOTO BY JIM COOPER OF SHARPBYCOOP.COM

Sean O'Hare

Splice | 2007

$7^{11}/_{16}$ X $^{11}/_{16}$ X $1^{1}/_{16}$ INCHES (19.5 X 1.7 X 2.8 CM)

Stainless Damascus steel, ironwood, 24-karat gold-plated screws; flat ground

PHOTO BY JIM COOPER OF SHARPBYCOOP.COM

D'Alton Holder

Plainsman and Rifleman | 2006

PLAINSMAN (LEFT), OVERALL LENGTH, 10¾ INCHES (27.3 CM)
RIFLEMAN (RIGHT), OVERALL LENGTH, 12¾ INCHES (32.3 CM)

ATS-34 steel, red maple, fossil manatee, paprika amber, white amber, oosic; engraved

ENGRAVED BY BRUCE SHAW AND BRUCE CHRISTENSEN
PHOTO BY JIM COOPER OF SHARPBYCOOP.COM

Joe Szilaski

Set of Presentation Tomahawks | 2005

HEADS, 8 1/4 INCHES (21 CM) EACH

W-2 tool steel, silver, hickory, deer antler; forged, engraved, inlaid, embellished

PHOTO BY JIM COOPER OF SHARPBYCOOP.COM

MICKE (Michael Andersson)

Untitled | 2007

11 3/8 X 9/16 X 1/4 INCHES (29 X 4 X 0.7 CM)

Spider-mosaic Damascus steel, oosic; forge welded

PHOTO BY ANDRÉ ANDERSSON

J.D. Smith

Large Bowie | 2007

OVERALL LENGTH, 15½ INCHES (39.4 CM)

Damascus steel, silver, wenge

PHOTO BY JIM COOPER OF SHARPBYCOOP.COM

Terry Knipschield

Wharn Cliffe | 2007

$^{11}/_{16}$ X $6^{5}/_{16}$ X $^{3}/_{8}$ INCHES (1.8 X 16 X 1 CM)

Damascus steel, mammoth ivory, titanium; anodized, stock removal, file worked

DAMASCUS BOLSTERS BY HOWARD CLARK
PHOTO BY MATT KNIPSCHIELD

Kaj Embretsen

Drop-Point Back-Lock Folder | 2006

Damascus steel, mammoth ivory scales, gold

PHOTO BY JIM COOPER OF SHARPBYCOOP.COM

Don Hanson III

Walrus Ivory Folder with Hamon | 2004

OVERALL LENGTH, 7 1/16 INCHES (18 CM)

1086 steel, mosaic Damascus steel, hamon, fossil walrus ivory, 18-karat rose gold, titanium; forged, file worked

PHOTO BY JIM COOPER OF SHARPBYCOOP.COM

Matthew Suddeth

Untitled | 2007

1 X 7 7/8 X 7/16 INCHES (2.5 X 20 X 1.2 CM)

Odin's-eye and gator-skin stainless Damascus steel, fossil mammoth ivory, opal

PHOTOS BY JANET C. LEMCKE

Maurie McCarthy

Art Knife | 2006

OVERALL LENGTH, 13 3/8 INCHES (34 CM)

Damascus steel, gold alloy, natural tortoiseshell, diamonds

PHOTO BY ARTIST

Don Hanson III

Giant Persian Latch-Release Folder | 2002

OVERALL LENGTH, 9 7/16 INCHES (24 CM)

Mosaic Damascus steel, fossil mammoth ivory, 18-karat rose gold, mother-of-pearl, titanium; forged, inlaid, file worked

PHOTO BY JIM COOPER OF SHARPBYCOOP.COM

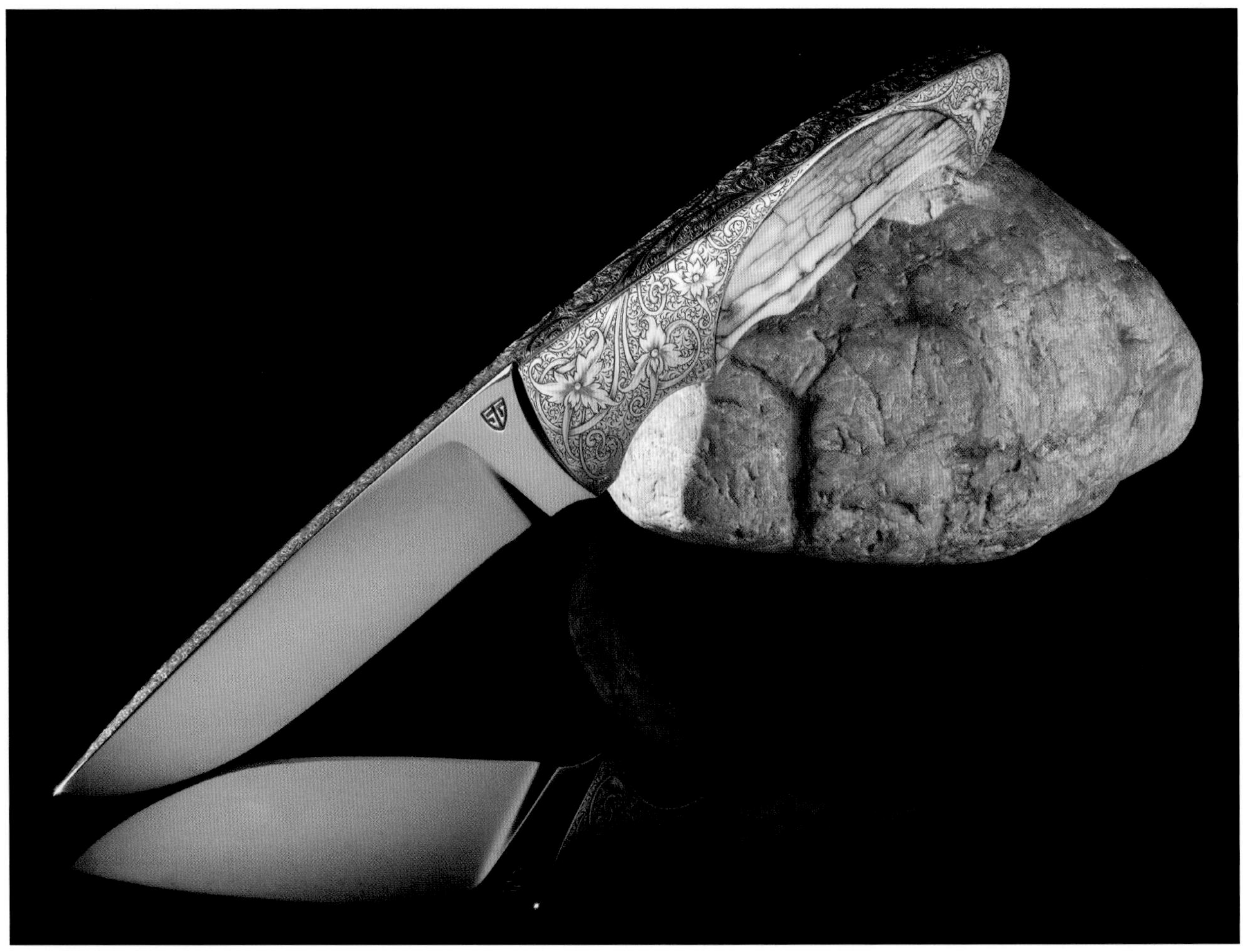

Stefan Gobec

Mammoth Flowers | 2005

1 5/16 X 10 13/16 X 2 15/16 INCHES (3.3 X 27.5 X 7.5 CM)

RWL-34 steel, mammoth ivory; engraved, polished

PHOTO BY ARTIST

Pat Crawford
Wes Crawford

Big Bite Kasper | 2007

OVERALL LENGTH, $9^1/_2$ INCHES (24 CM)

Stainless Damascus steel, mammoth tooth, titanium; file worked, engine turned, anodized

PHOTO BY JIM COOPER OF SHARPBYCOOP.COM

Francesco Pachí

Little Tanto | 2000

OVERALL LENGTH, $6\frac{5}{8}$ INCHES (16.9 CM)

Carbon Damascus steel, tiger coral, 18-karat gold

PHOTO BY ARTIST

Larry Lunn

Tortoise Shell D/A | 2006

OVERALL LENGTH, 9 1/2 INCHES (24.1 CM)

Spirograph Damascus steel, sculpted-lace Damascus steel, estate tortoiseshell, ebony, champagne diamond, vermeil button, diamonds

PHOTO BY JIM COOPER OF SHARPBYCOOP.COM

Darriel K. Caston

The Twins | 2007

EACH, 2¾ X ½ X 1 15/16 INCHES (7 X 1.3 X 5 CM)

AEB-L stainless steel, Damascus steel, titanium, antique tortoiseshell; carved

DAMASCUS STEEL BY DILBERT EALY
PHOTO BY JIM COOPER OF SHARPBYCOOP.COM

Bill Saindon

Latch-Release Side-Lock Folder | 2003

OVERALL LENGTH, 8½ INCHES (21.6 CM)

Damascus steel, mosaic Damascus steel, fossil walrus ivory, titanium, 18-karat gold; colored, carved, file worked, inlaid

MOSAIC DAMASCUS STEEL BY HANK KNICKMEYER AND TODD KINNIKIN
DAMASCUS STEEL BY ROBERT EGGERLING
PHOTO BY JIM COOPER OF SHARPBYCOOP.COM

Don Hanson III

Denim-Blue Damascus Folder | 2003

OVERALL LENGTH, 6 7/8 INCHES (17.5 CM)

Mosaic Damascus steel, fossil mammoth ivory, 18-karat rose gold, titanium; forged, file worked

PHOTO BY JIM COOPER OF SHARPBYCOOP.COM

Allen Elishewitz

Timascus Scout | 2007

1 3/16 X 9 1/16 X 7/16 INCHES (3 X 23 X 1.2 CM)

Titanium-based Damascus steel, black-lip pearl, white diamonds, stainless steel, titanium; drilled, machine cut

PHOTO BY VALERIE ELISHEWITZ

Johan Gustafsson

Mosaic Fighter | 2003

OVERALL LENGTH, 19 11/16 INCHES (50 CM)

Mosaic Damascus steel, gold, walrus ivory; forge welded, drilled, heat-treated, polished

PHOTO BY POINTSEVEN STUDIOS

Barry Gallagher

Mosaic Raptor | 2006

OVERALL LENGTH, 8 INCHES (20.3 CM)

Mosaic Damascus steel, black-lip pearl, 1084 steel, sapphires; carved, textured, file worked

PHOTO BY JIM COOPER OF SHARPBYCOOP.COM

Bill Saindon

Latch-Release Side-Lock Symmetrical Dagger | 2003

OVERALL LENGTH, 9 INCHES (22.9 CM)

Damascus steel, antique tortoise shell, 18-karat gold, titanium; colored, carved, file worked, inlaid

DAMASCUS STEEL BY ROBERT EGGERLING
PHOTO BY JIM COOPER OF SHARPBYCOOP.COM

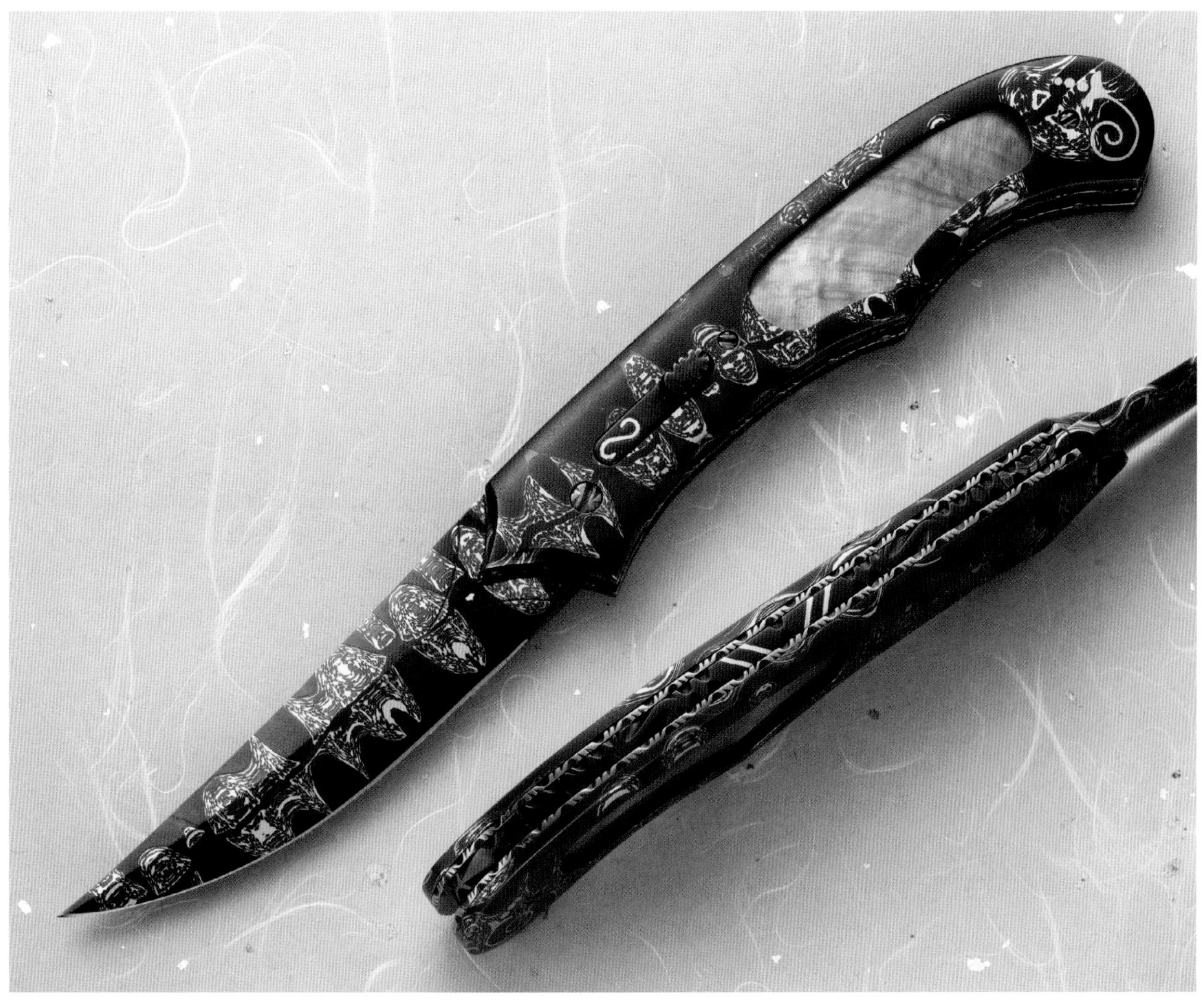

Rick Dunkerley

Persian Auto | 2005

Damascus steel, 1018 steel, 24-karat gold, sapphire; engraved, inlaid, file worked, nitre blued, set

PHOTO BY POINTSEVEN STUDIOS

Lloyd Hale

Golden Fans | 2004

440C stainless steel, gold-lip pearl, abalone

PHOTO BY JIM COOPER OF SHARPBYCOOP.COM

Koji Hara

Mizigumo | 2001

OVERALL LENGTH, 5 3/8 INCHES (13.7 CM)

Cowry-Y steel, 420 stainless steel, diamond, mother-of-pearl; carved, inlaid, polished

PHOTO BY JIM COOPER OF SHARPBYCOOP.COM

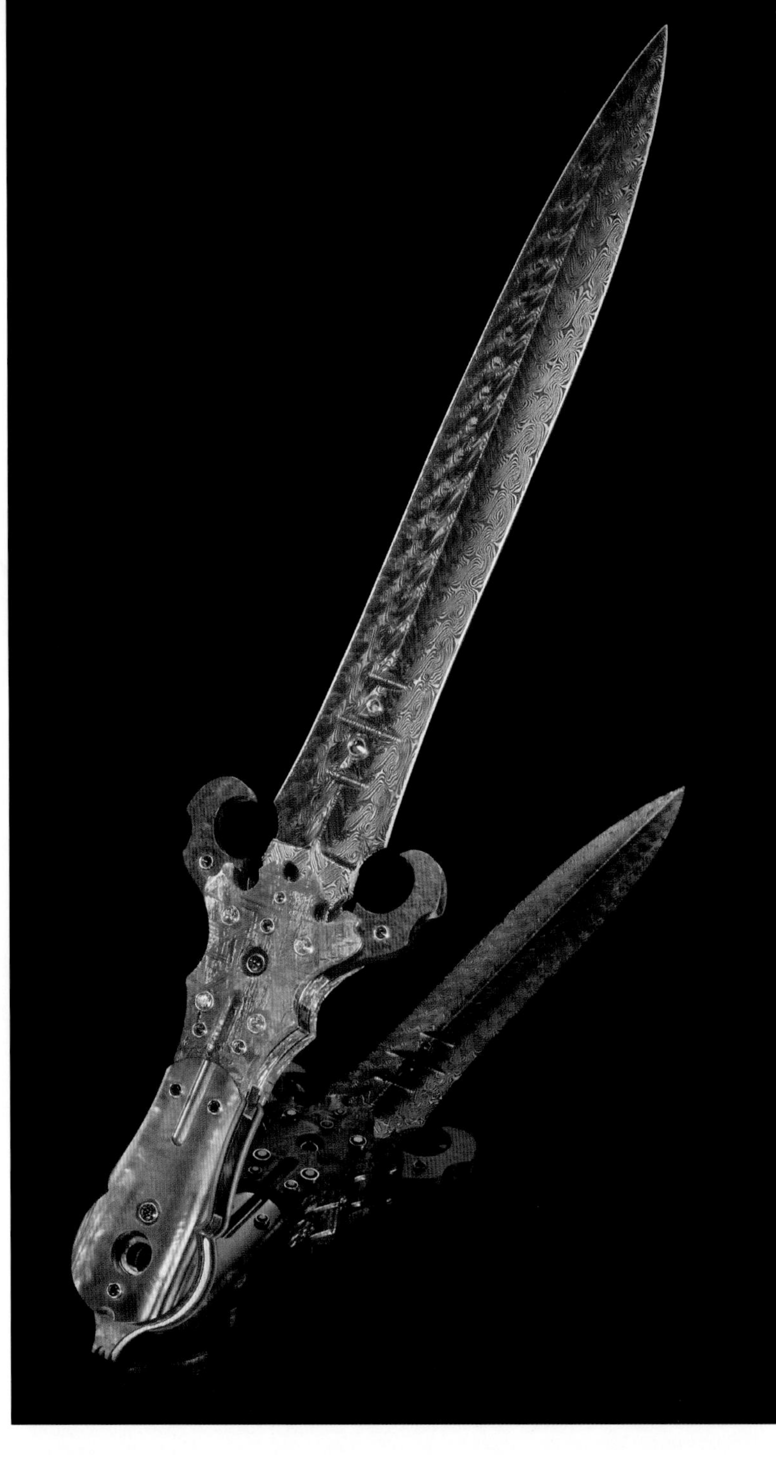

John L. Jensen

Nuibiru | 2008

OVERALL LENGTH, $8^1/_2$ INCHES (21.6 CM)

Turkish-twist Damascus, 22-karat gold, 18-karat gold, titanium, peridot, amethyst, Gibeon meteorite, black-lip pearl, iolites, garnets, abalone; hollow ground, etched, blued, chemically colored

PHOTO BY JESSICA MARCOTTE

George E. Dailey

Folding Bowie | 2001

OVERALL LENGTH, 8 1/2 INCHES (21.6 CM)

Clad Damascus steel, diamonds, 18-karat gold, mother-of-pearl, titanium; anodized

DAMASCUS BY DARYL MEIER
PHOTO BY JIM COOPER OF SHARPBYCOOP.COM

Johan Gustafsson

Symphony | 2005

OVERALL LENGTH, 7⅞ INCHES (20 CM)

Mosaic Damascus steel, mother-of-pearl, gold-plated screws, rubies; forge welded, drilled, heat-treated, polished

PHOTO BY JIM COOPER OF SHARPBYCOOP.COM

Harumi Hirayama

Pico Series Rear-Lock Folders: Dragonfly and Butterfly | 2004

DRAGONFLY KNIFE, 6 5/16 X 1 3/16 X 11/16 INCHES (16 X 3 X 1.8 CM)
BUTTERFLY KNIFE, 5 1/4 X 7/8 X 9/16 INCHES (13.3 X 2.3 X 1.5 CM)

440C stainless steel, silver, 18-karat gold, ironwood, shell, coral, stone; engraved, inlaid

PHOTO BY TOMO HASEGAWA

Pat Crawford
Wes Crawford

Point Guard | 2007

OVERALL LENGTH, 10 INCHES (25.5 CM)

S30V steel, Damascus steel, titanium, abalone; file worked, engine turned, anodized

PHOTO BY JIM COOPER OF SHARPBYCOOP.COM

Scot Matsuoka

Pahinui | 2007

OVERALL LENGTH, 8 INCHES (20.3 CM)

CPM-154 steel, titanium, camel bone; anodized, inlaid, file worked

PHOTO BY JIM COOPER OF SHARPBYCOOP.COM

Jim Minnick
Joyce Minnick
Mermaid | 2003

OVERALL LENGTH, 8½ INCHES (21.6 CM)

Turkish-twist Damascus steel, stainless steel, 24-karat gold, diamond, blue quartz; carved, inlaid, engraved

DAMASCUS STEEL BY JERRY RADOS
PHOTO BY POINTSEVEN STUDIOS

Brian Tighe

Twist Tighe Nouveau | 2007

BLADE, 3 5/8 INCHES (9.2 CM)

Stainless Damascus steel, titanium; engraved

PHOTO BY POINTSEVEN STUDIOS

Shane Taylor

Dreams of Shalott | 2005

3 1/4 X 1/2 X 3/16 INCHES (8.3 X 1.3 X 0.5 CM)

Image mosaic Damascus steel, mammoth ivory, abalone, gold; inlaid, engraved

PHOTO BY POINTSEVEN STUDIOS

Reinhard Tschager

Small Pocket Drop | 2007

OVERALL LENGTH, 4 15/16 INCHES (12.5 CM)

Damascus steel, ivory, 18-karat gold; engraved

DAMASCUS BY BERTIE RIETVELD
PHOTO BY FRANCESCO PACHÍ

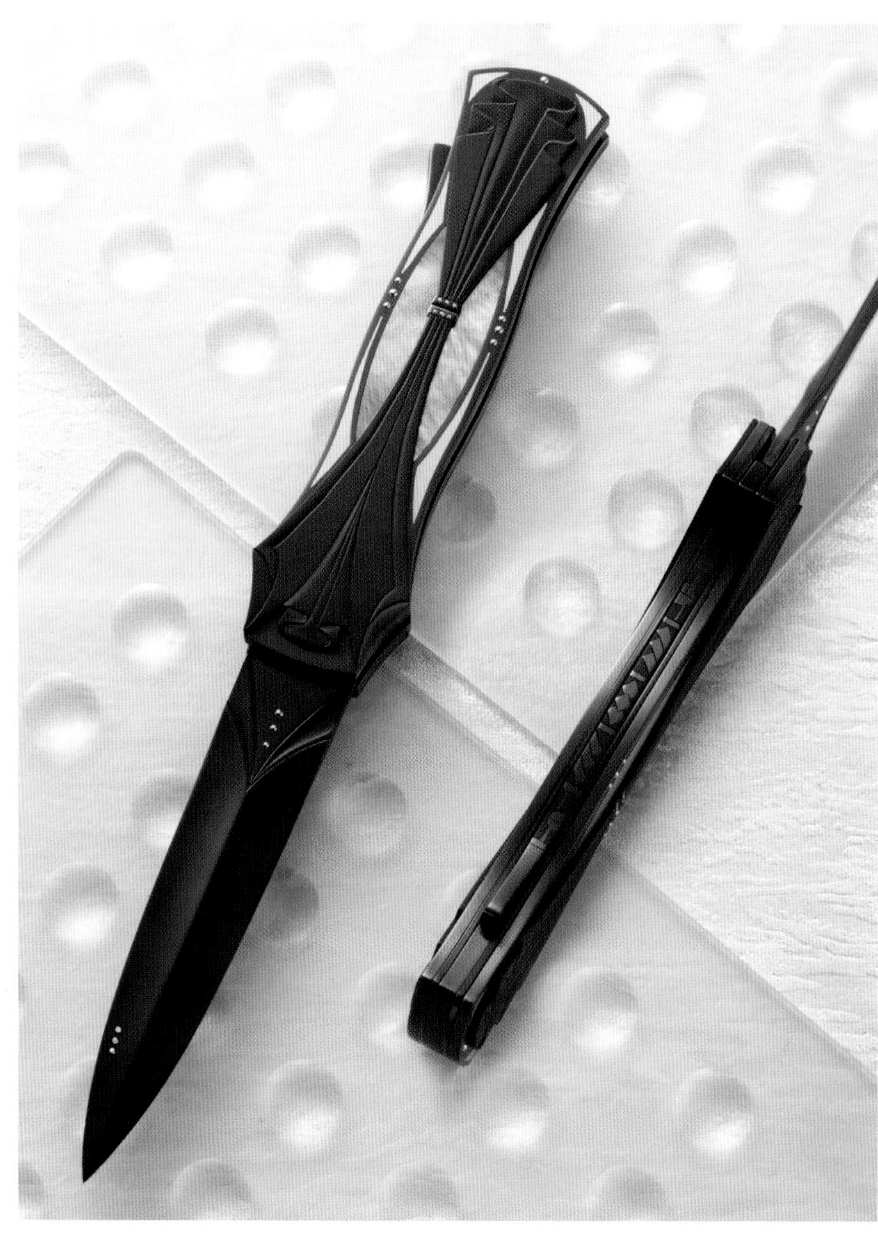

Jim Minnick
Joyce Minnick
Calypso | 2005
OVERALL LENGTH, 8½ INCHES (21.6 CM)
Steel, mother-of-pearl, 24-karat gold, titanium; anodized, blued, carved, inlaid
PHOTO BY POINTSEVEN STUDIOS

Warren Osborne

Model 28 | 2003

BLADE, 4 INCHES (10.2 CM)

Stainless Damascus steel, 14-karat gold; file worked

DAMASCUS STEEL BY MIKE NORRIS
PHOTO BY JIM COOPER OF SHARPBYCOOP.COM

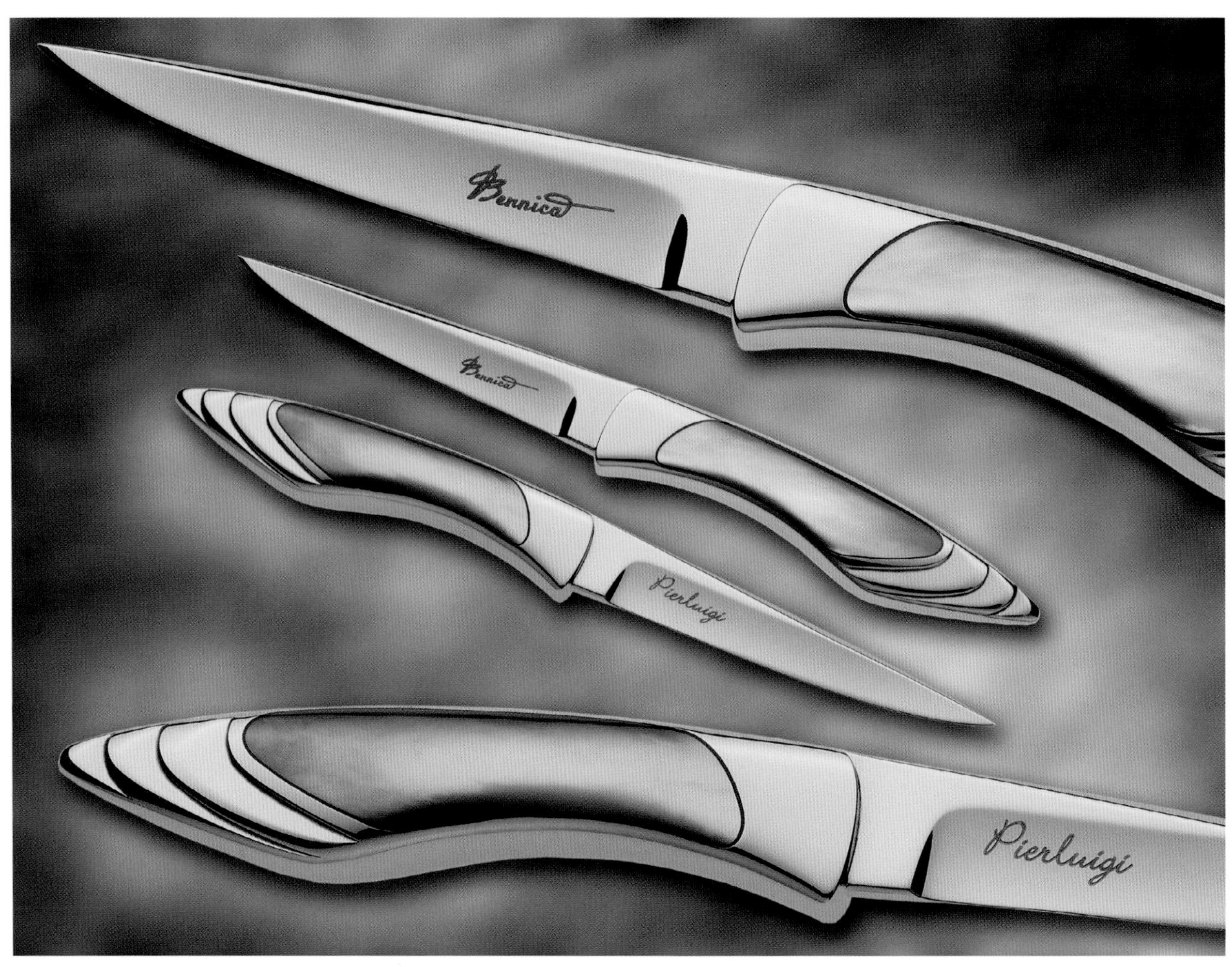

Charlie Bennica

Pierluigi Miniature | 2002

OVERALL LENGTH, 4 5/16 INCHES (11 CM)

RWL-34 steel, 416 stainless steel, black pearl; sculpted

PHOTO BY FRANCESCO PACHÍ

Owen Wood

Batwing Folding Knife | 2006

OVERALL LENGTH, 6 1/2 INCHES (16.5 CM)

Pinstripe and explosion composite Damascus steel, 416 stainless steel, 303 stainless steel, black-lip pearl, titanium; decorated, blued, engraved

ENGRAVED BY JON ROBYN
PHOTO BY JIM COOPER OF SHARPBYCOOP.COM

Warren Osborne

Large Model 27B Inter-Frame | 2004

OVERALL LENGTH, 7⁷⁄₈ INCHES (20 CM)

Stainless Damascus steel, gold-lip mother-of-pearl, 14-karat gold; inlaid

DAMASCUS STEEL BY MIKE NORRIS
PHOTO BY JIM COOPER OF SHARPBYCOOP.COM

Arpád Bojtoš

Hercules and the Hydra | 2007

OVERALL LENGTH, $9^{13}/_{16}$ INCHES (25 CM)

440C stainless steel, mammoth ivory, hippopotamus ivory, snakewood, silver, gold

PHOTO BY POINTSEVEN STUDIOS

Wade Colter

The Goblin Gun | 2003

OVERALL LENGTH, 11 1/2 INCHES (29.2 CM)

Ladder-pattern Damascus steel, mule deer antler; nitre blued, hand forged, carved

PHOTO BY POINTSEVEN STUDIOS

Robert Weinstock

Untitled | 2006

OVERALL LENGTH, 6 3/16 INCHES (15.8 CM)

Damascus steel, 14-karat gold; carved, chased

PHOTO BY ARTIST

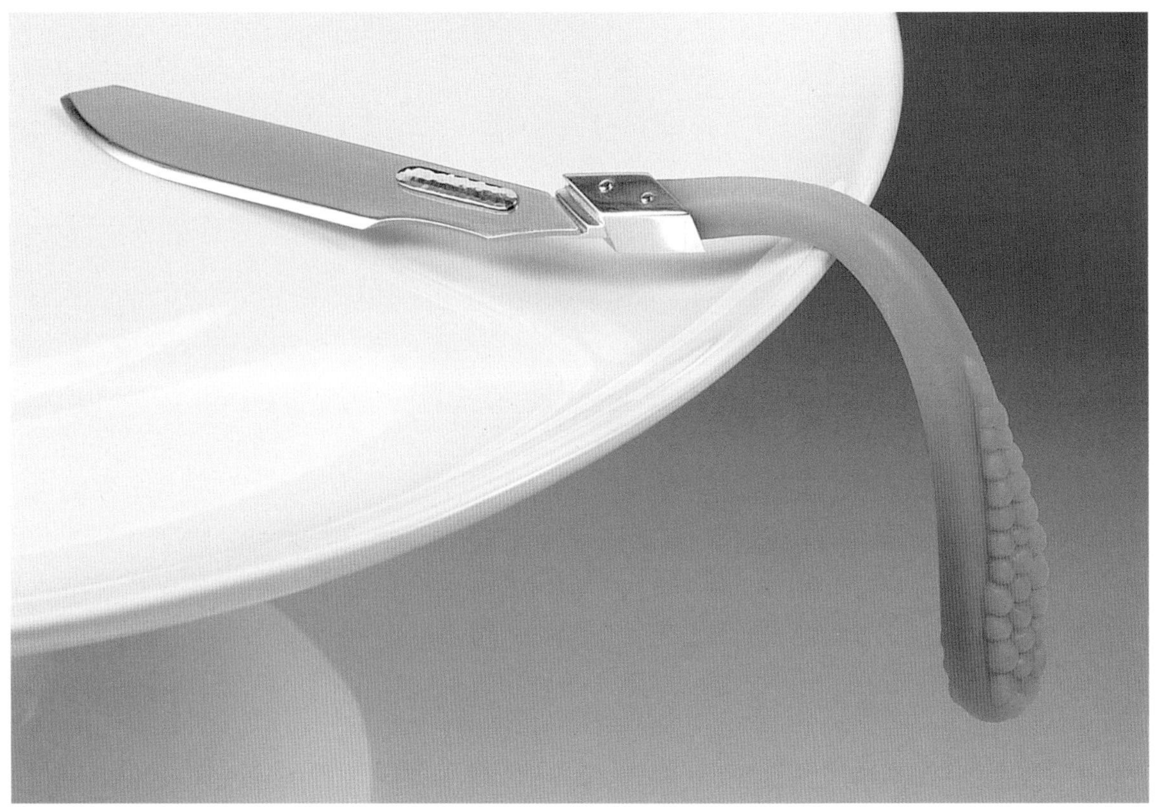

Lilyana Bekic

Adipose Knife | 2006

OVERALL LENGTH, 8 7/8 INCHES (22.6 CM)

Stainless steel, fine silver, silicone rubber; fabricated, cast

PHOTO BY ARTIST

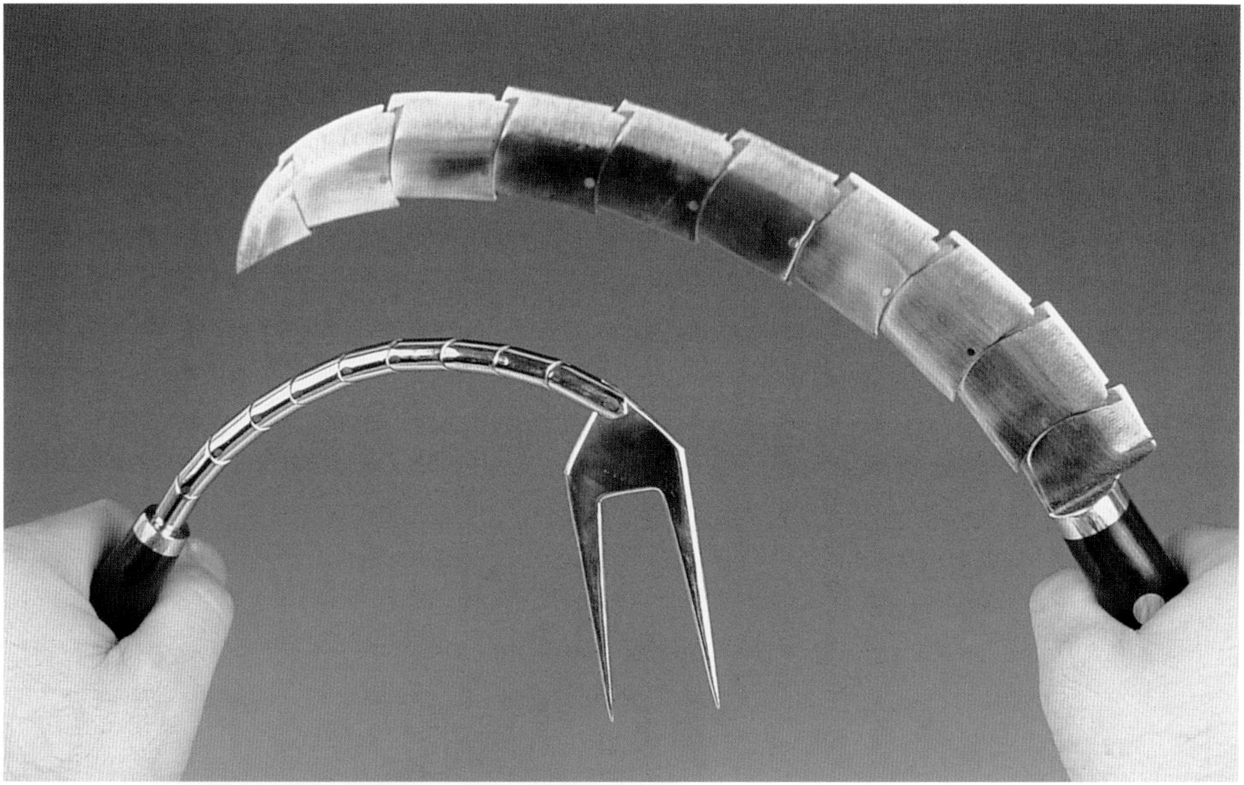

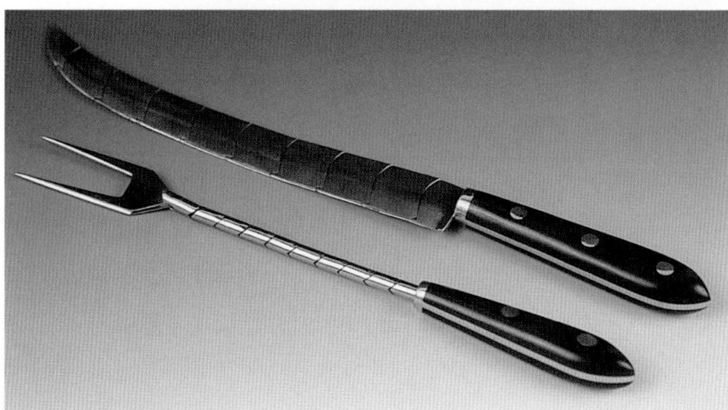

Rebecca Scheer

Futensils: Carving Set | 2000

FORK, $11\frac{15}{16}$ X $1\frac{5}{16}$ X $\frac{11}{16}$ INCHES (30.4 X 3.3 X 1.8 CM);
KNIFE, $13\frac{15}{16}$ X $1\frac{1}{2}$ X $\frac{11}{16}$ INCHES (35.5 X 3.8 X 1.8 CM)

Mild steel, brass, ebony; CNC lathed, hand constructed

PHOTOS BY ARTIST

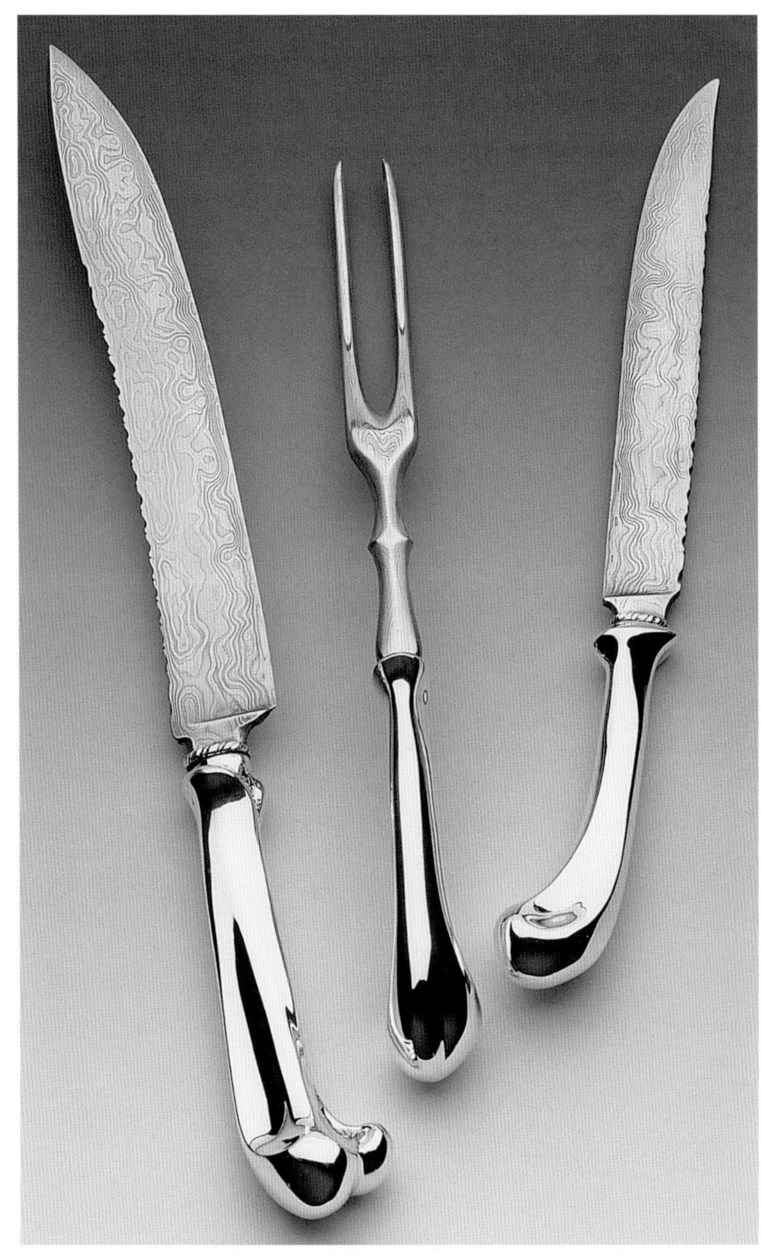

Wendy Yothers

Damascus Weapons for Dining | 2000

LARGEST KNIFE, 14 15/16 X 1 3/16 X 3/4 INCHES (38 X 3 X 2 CM); FORK AND KNIFE, 11 13/16 X 3/4 X 3/8 INCHES (30 X 2 X 1 CM) EACH

Damascus steel, sterling silver, 24-karat gold; hand forged, sculpted, cast

PHOTOS BY RICHARD DUANE

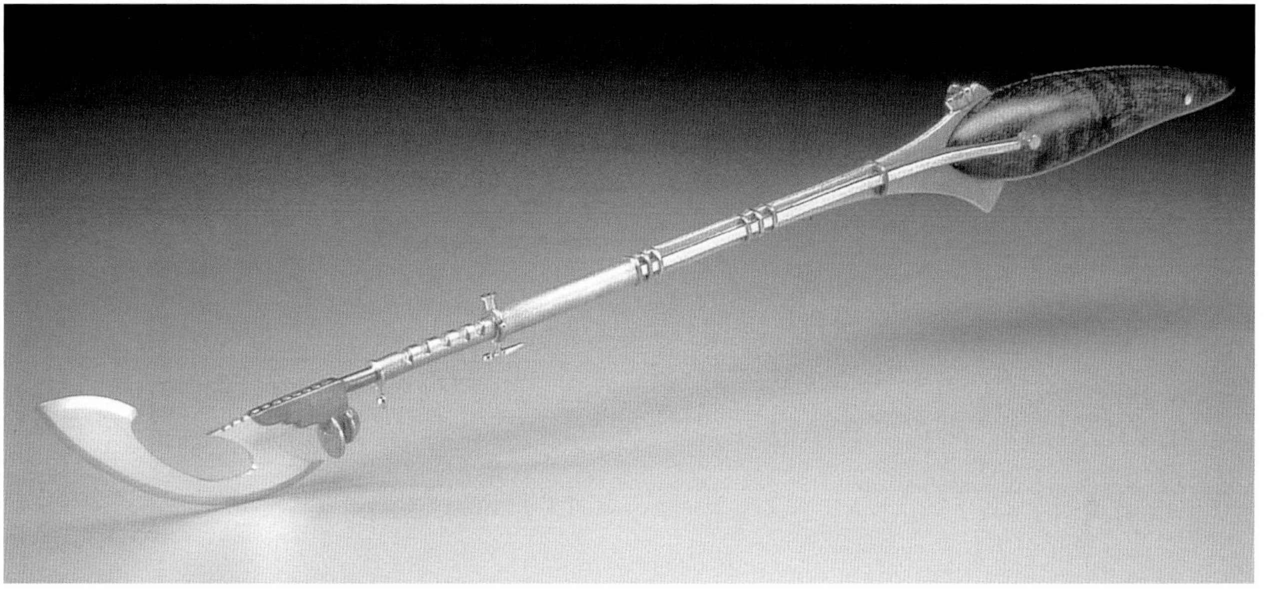

Tom Ferrero

Instrument | 2007

$1\frac{3}{16}$ X $10\frac{1}{4}$ X $1\frac{3}{16}$ INCHES (3 X 26 X 3 CM)

Silver, 22-karat gold, copper, blue zircon, tanzanite, black mulga wood, patina; hand fabricated, carved, riveted

PHOTO BY KEVIN MONTAGUE

Isabelle Posillico
"Eat" Cheese Knives | 2007
$2^{3}/_{8}$ X $2^{3}/_{8}$ X $4^{5}/_{16}$ INCHES (6 X 6 X 11 CM)
Sterling silver; roller printed, hammered, formed
PHOTO BY HAP SAKWA

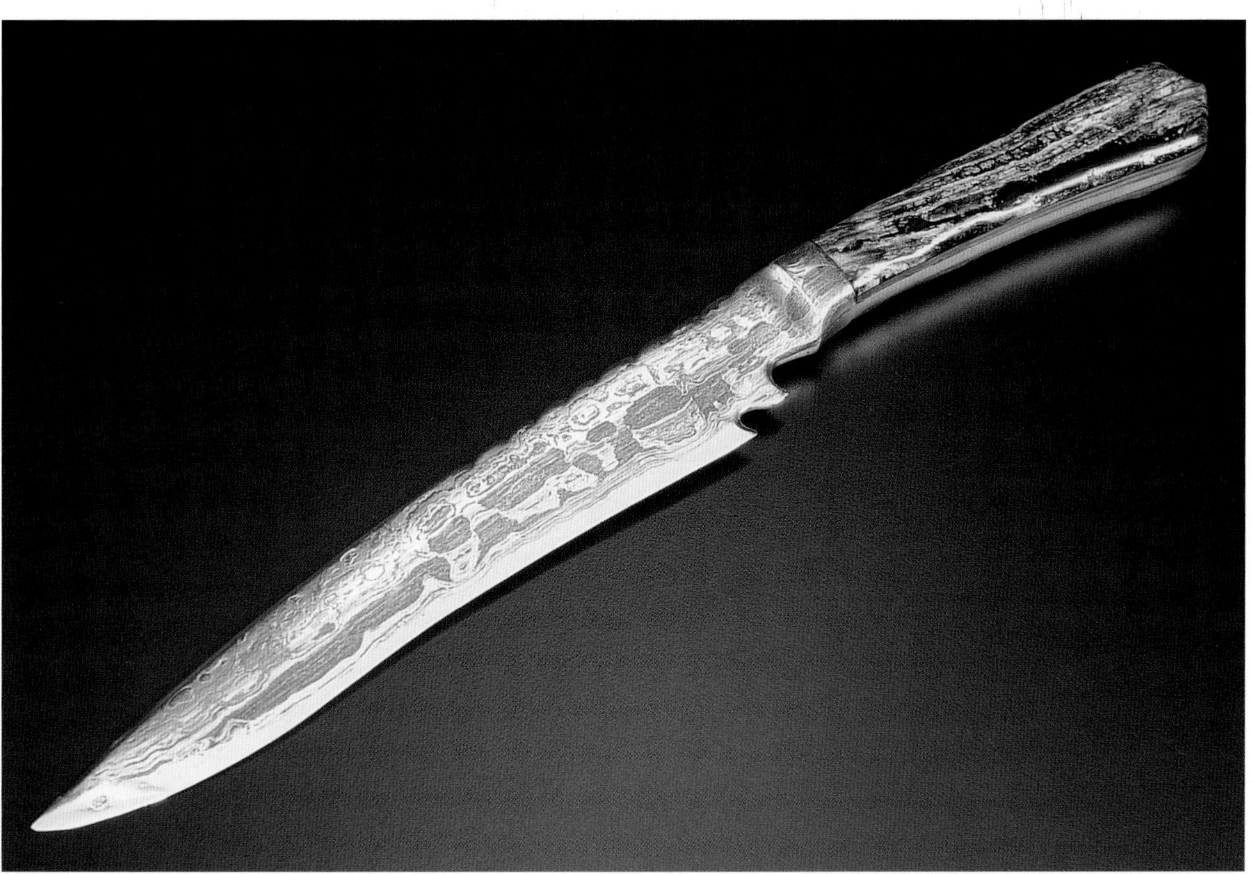

Robert Coogan

Land Shark | 2007

1 9/16 X 15 3/4 X 1 INCHES (4 X 40 X 2.5 CM)

Steel, iron, dinosaur tooth; fabricated, forge welded

PHOTO BY TTU PHOTO SERVICES

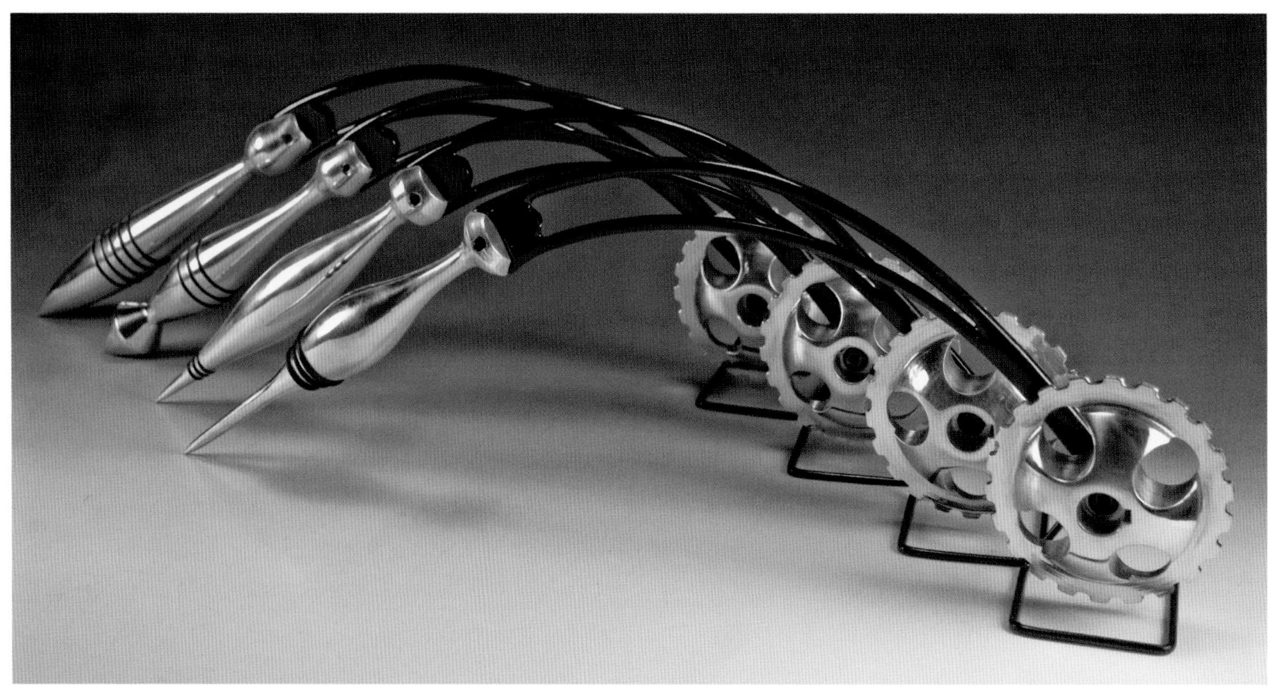

Frankie Flood

Stinger #4 Pizza Cutter | 2007

6¼ X 17½ X 2¼ INCHES (15.9 X 44.5 X 5.7 CM)

Aluminum, steel, bronze; lathed, welded, powder coated

PHOTO BY ARTIST

Yi-Shin Liu

Transition I (Petite Knife) | 2003

$3/4$ X $3/16$ X $4\,5/16$ INCHES (2 X 0.5 X 11 CM)

Sterling silver; forged

PHOTO BY ARTIST

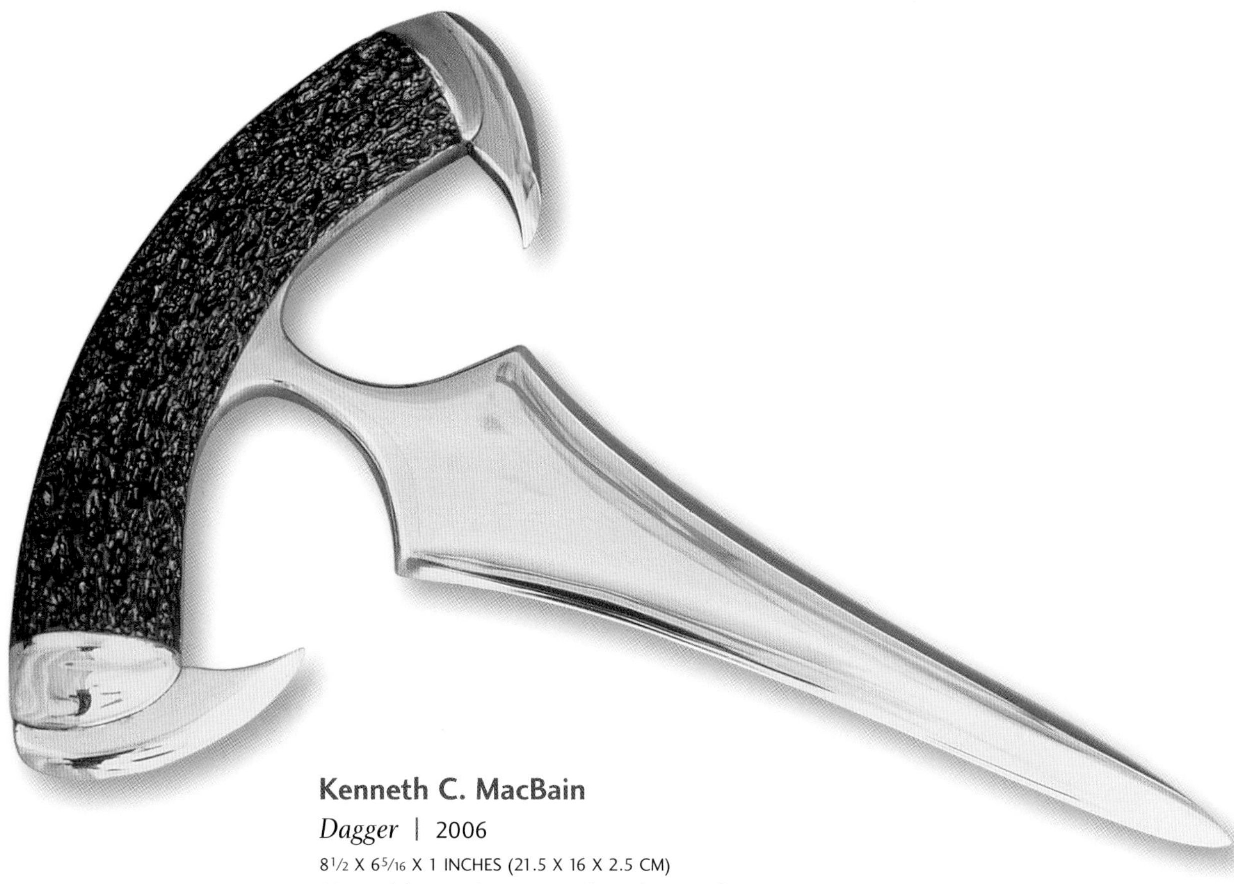

Kenneth C. MacBain

Dagger | 2006

$8^{1}/_{2}$ X $6^{5}/_{16}$ X 1 INCHES (21.5 X 16 X 2.5 CM)

01 steel, brass, ebony, resin; forged, ground, cast

PHOTO BY ARTIST

Wade Colter

Goblin Multi-Blade | 2002

OVERALL LENGTH, 12 INCHES (30.5 CM)

Ladder-pattern Damascus steel, mule deer antler; forged, nitre blued, carved

PHOTO BY POINTSEVEN STUDIOS

R.J. Martin

Dress Havoc Flipper | 2004

OVERALL LENGTH, 7 7/8 INCHES (20 CM)

CPM-S30V steel, titanium, carbon fiber, roller-thrust bearings

PHOTO BY JIM COOPER OF SHARPBYCOOP.COM

Matthew Lerch

Titan | 2007

OVERALL LENGTH, 6¾ INCHES (17 CM)

S30V steel, titanium; engraved, textured

ENGRAVED AND TEXTURED BY MARY JO LERCH
PHOTO BY JIM COOPER OF SHARPBYCOOP.COM

R.J. Martin

Devastator and *Havoc* | 2004

DEVASTATOR (LEFT), OVERALL LENGTH, 9½ INCHES (24.1 CM)
HAVOC (RIGHT), OVERALL LENGTH, 8 INCHES (20.3 CM)

CMP-S30V steel, titanium, roller-thrust bearings; faceted

PHOTO BY JIM COOPER OF SHARPBYCOOP.COM

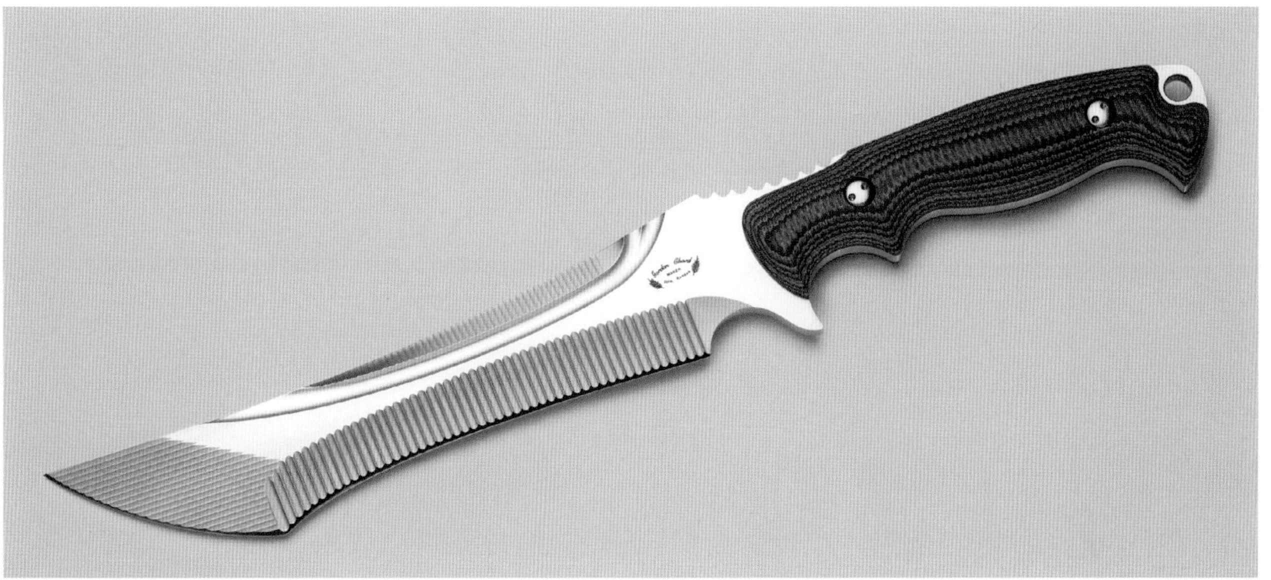

Gordon R. Chard

Millennium Fighter | 2007

12 X 1 3/4 X 3/16 INCHES (30.5 X 4.5 X 0.5 CM)

440C stainless steel, G10 steel, stainless steel; heat-treated, stained

PHOTO BY DAVID HOPKINS

Brent Sandow

Paratrooper | 2007

1 15/16 X 9/16 X 9 13/16 INCHES (5 X 1.5 X 25 CM)

Micarta, non-reflective coating; tang constructed

PHOTO BY NORMAN SANDOW

Sal Manaro

Hole Shot | 2004

$1\frac{9}{16}$ X $\frac{7}{8}$ X $\frac{3}{16}$ INCHES (4 X 2.3 X 0.5 CM)

ATS-34 steel, titanium

PHOTO BY JIM COOPER OF SHARPBYCOOP.COM

Matt Cucchiara

El Dorado Flipper | 2008

OVERALL LENGTH, 9 INCHES (22.9 CM)

Damascus steel, titanium, CPM 154 steel; hand carved, anodized, hand rubbed

PHOTO BY JIM COOPER OF SHARPBYCOOP.COM

Keith Ouye

Dead Man's Hand | 2006

OVERALL LENGTH, 9 INCHES (22.9 CM)

ATS-34 stainless steel, 6AL4V titanium; engraved, heat-treated

ENGRAVED BY C.J. CAI
HEAT-TREATED BY PAUL BOS
PHOTO BY JIM COOPER OF SHARPBYCOOP.COM

Kaj Embretsen

Eight-Piece Multi-Bladed Slip-Joint Folder | 2006

DIMENSIONS VARIABLE

Damascus steel, gold; hand filed

PHOTO BY JIM COOPER OF SHARPBYCOOP.COM

Ron Newton

Pistol Knife | 2002

3 X 1 X 9 INCHES (7.6 X 2.5 X 22.9 CM)

Mosaic Damascus steel, twist Damascus steel, ebony, sterling silver, 24-karat gold, bullet box; inlaid

PHOTO BY POINTSEVEN STUDIOS

Warren Osborne

Model 28 Inter-Frame | 2006

OVERALL LENGTH, 7 1/8 INCHES (18.1 CM)

CPM-154 stainless steel, 416 stainless steel, jasper, 14-karat gold; inlaid

PHOTO BY JIM COOPER OF SHARPBYCOOP.COM

Steve W. Hoel

Medium Coke Bottle | 1998

BLADE, $3\frac{1}{8}$ INCHES (7.9 CM)

ATS-34 stainless steel, 416 stainless steel, rosewood, paua shell; heat-treated, inlaid

PHOTO BY JIM COOPER OF SHARPBYCOOP.COM

Rob Brown

145 Clip-Point Hunter | 2007

OVERALL LENGTH, 10 9/16 INCHES (26.8 CM)

ATS-34 steel, 303 stainless steel, Arizona desert ironwood; hand ground, mirror polished

PHOTO BY JIM COOPER OF SHARPBYCOOP.COM

Steven R. Johnson

Mediterranean Dirk | 2007

OVERALL LENGTH, $12\frac{3}{16}$ INCHES (31 CM)

ATS-34 steel, 416 stainless steel, sambar stag

PHOTO BY JIM COOPER OF SHARPBYCOOP.COM

MICKE (Michael Andersson)

Untitled | 2007

$12^{9}/_{16}$ X $1^{9}/_{16}$ X $^{1}/_{4}$ INCHES (32 X 4 X 0.7 CM)

Twist and explosion Damascus steel, copper, mammoth ivory; forge welded

PHOTO BY ANDRÉ ANDERSSON

Rob Brown

188 Camp Knife | 2007

OVERALL LENGTH, 12 1/4 INCHES (31.2 CM)

ATS-34 steel, 303 stainless steel, mastodon ivory; hand ground, mirror polished

PHOTO BY JIM COOPER OF SHARPBYCOOP.COM

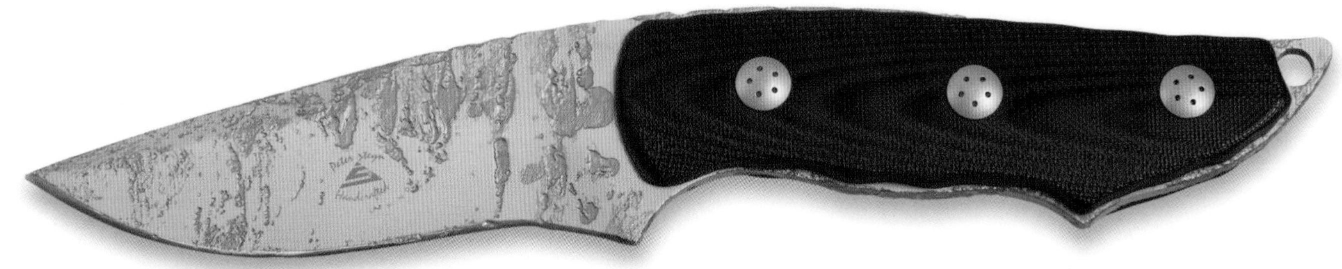

Peter Steyn

Crator | 2007

9 1/4 X 1 5/8 X 5/8 INCHES (23.5 X 4.2 X 1.6 CM)

G10 steel, stainless steel, 12C27 steel; bead blasted, crator finished

PHOTO BY KEN SMYTH

John White

Damascus Ladder-Pattern "W" Southwest Bowie | 2007

OVERALL LENGTH, 13¼ INCHES (33.7 CM)

Damascus steel, nickel silver, African blackwood, fine silver; forged, grooved, fabricated, file worked

PHOTO BY POINTSEVEN STUDIOS

Dusty Moulton

The Silverado | 2006

OVERALL LENGTH, 11 1/2 INCHES (29.2 CM)

CPM 154CM steel, 416 stainless steel; engraved

PHOTO BY KNIFEART.COM

Russ Sutton

Flowing Texture | 2007

5 11/16 X 1 X 9/16 INCHES (14.5 X 2.5 X 1.5 CM)

Stainless Damascus steel, 416 stainless steel, mammoth ivory, 18-karat gold, natural ruby; engraved

DAMASCUS STEEL BY MIKE NORRIS
PHOTO BY ARTIST

David Broadwell

Engraved Persian Fighter | 2004

OVERALL LENGTH, 14 INCHES (35.5 CM)

Twist Damascus steel, bronze, red mallee burl; carved, engraved, hollow ground, flat ground, textured, stock removal

ENGRAVED BY RAY COVER
PHOTO BY JIM COOPER OF SHARPBYCOOP.COM

Sean O'Hare

Hunter-B | 2006

$9^{11}/_{16}$ X $^{11}/_{16}$ X $1^{3}/_{8}$ INCHES (24.7 X 1.7 X 3.5 CM)

S30V steel, 416 stainless steel, juniper burl, mosaic pins; flat ground, mirror finished, engraved

ENGRAVED BY BRUCE SHAW
PHOTO BY JIM COOPER OF SHARPBYCOOP.COM

Ronald Best

Untitled | 2007

OVERALL LENGTH, $20^{1}/_{16}$ INCHES (50 CM)

440C stainless steel, ivory; hand carved

PHOTO BY JIM COOPER OF SHARPBYCOOP.COM

Mick Penfold

Samuel Bell-Style Bowie | 2003

OVERALL LENGTH, 14 15/16 INCHES (38 CM)

Ebony, nickel silver; engraved

ENGRAVED BY JIM WHITEHEAD
PHOTO BY RAUSIN

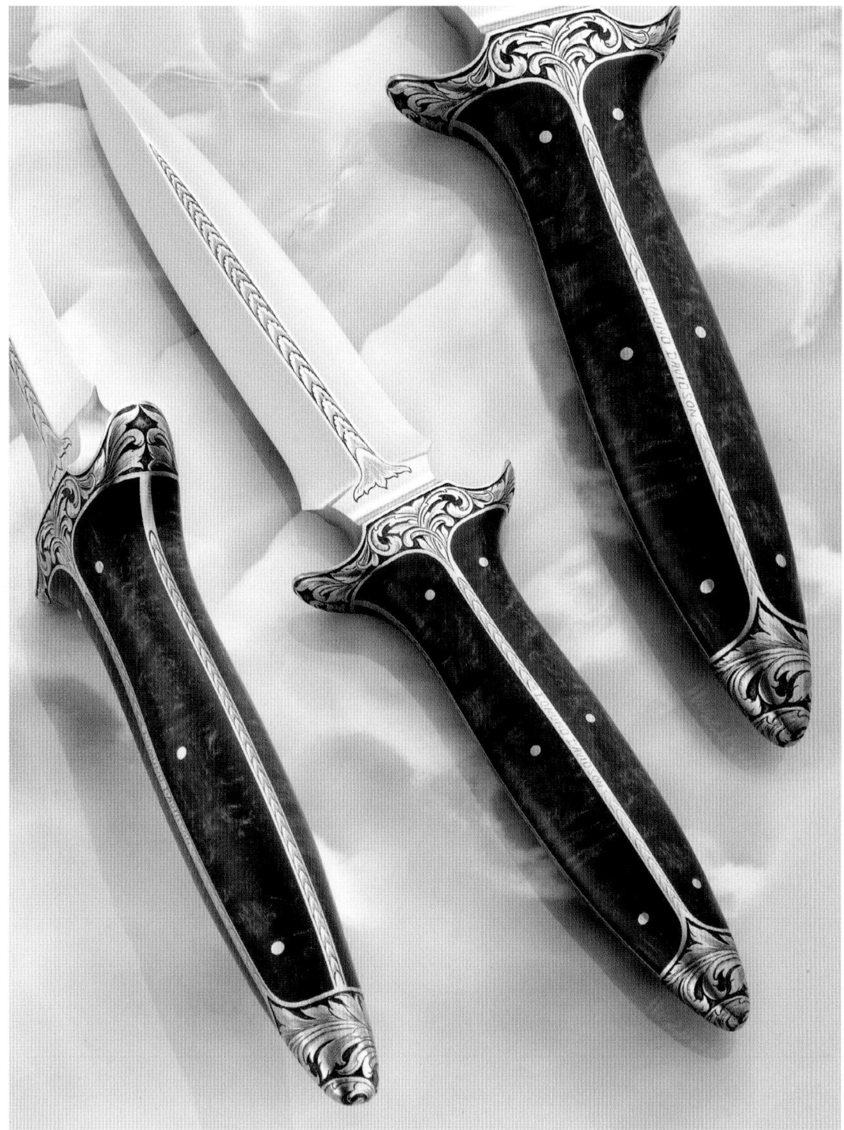

Edmund Davidson

Von Karl's Death Star Dagger | 2004

OVERALL LENGTH, 12¼ INCHES (31.1 CM)

440C stainless steel, desert ironwood; engraved, heat-treated, integral constructed

ENGRAVED BY JERE DAVIDSON
HEAT-TREATED BY PAUL BOS
PHOTO BY POINTSEVEN STUDIOS

Don Lozier

Untitled (Boot Dagger) | 2007

OVERALL LENGTH, 7 7/8 INCHES (20 CM)

Stainless raindrop-pattern Damascus steel, 416 stainless steel

DAMASCUS BY MIKE NORRIS
PHOTO BY JIM COOPER OF SHARPBYCOOP.COM

Sherry Cordova

Khanjar Letter Opener | 2007

6 7/16 X 1 13/16 X 3/4 INCHES (16.4 X 4.6 X 2 CM)

Fine silver, sterling silver; hand fabricated, filigreed

PHOTO BY ARTIST

Steven R. Johnson

Loveless-Style Big Bear Fighter | 2001

OVERALL LENGTH, $14\frac{3}{16}$ INCHES (36 CM)

ATS-34 steel, 416 stainless steel, mother-of-pearl; engraved

ENGRAVED BY STEVE LINDSAY
PHOTO BY POINTSEVEN STUDIOS

Dennis E. Friedly

Gent's Blue Bowie | 2007

OVERALL LENGTH, 11 1/2 INCHES (29.3 CM)

ATS-34 steel, gold, diamonds; gun blued, nitre blued, engraved, inlaid, set

ENGRAVED BY GIL RUDOLPH
PHOTO BY POINTSEVEN STUDIOS

Terry Knipschield

Persian | 2007

3/4 X 7 7/16 X 9/16 INCHES (2 X 19 X 1.5 CM)

Stainless bubble wrap-pattern Damascus steel, mosaic Damascus steel, mother-of-pearl, titanium; anodized, stock removal, file worked

DAMASCUS BLADE BY DEVIN THOMAS
MOSAIC DAMASCUS BOLSTERS BY CHRIS MARKS
PHOTO BY MATT KNIPSCHIELD

Aad van Rijswijk (AVR Knives)

Ramses | 2001

OVERALL LENGTH, 6 1/2 INCHES (16.5 CM)

Stainless rose-pattern Damascus steel, ATS-34 steel, lapis lazuli, 24-karat white gold, 24-karat yellow gold; engraved, inlaid

PHOTO BY BOB VAN TIENHOVEN

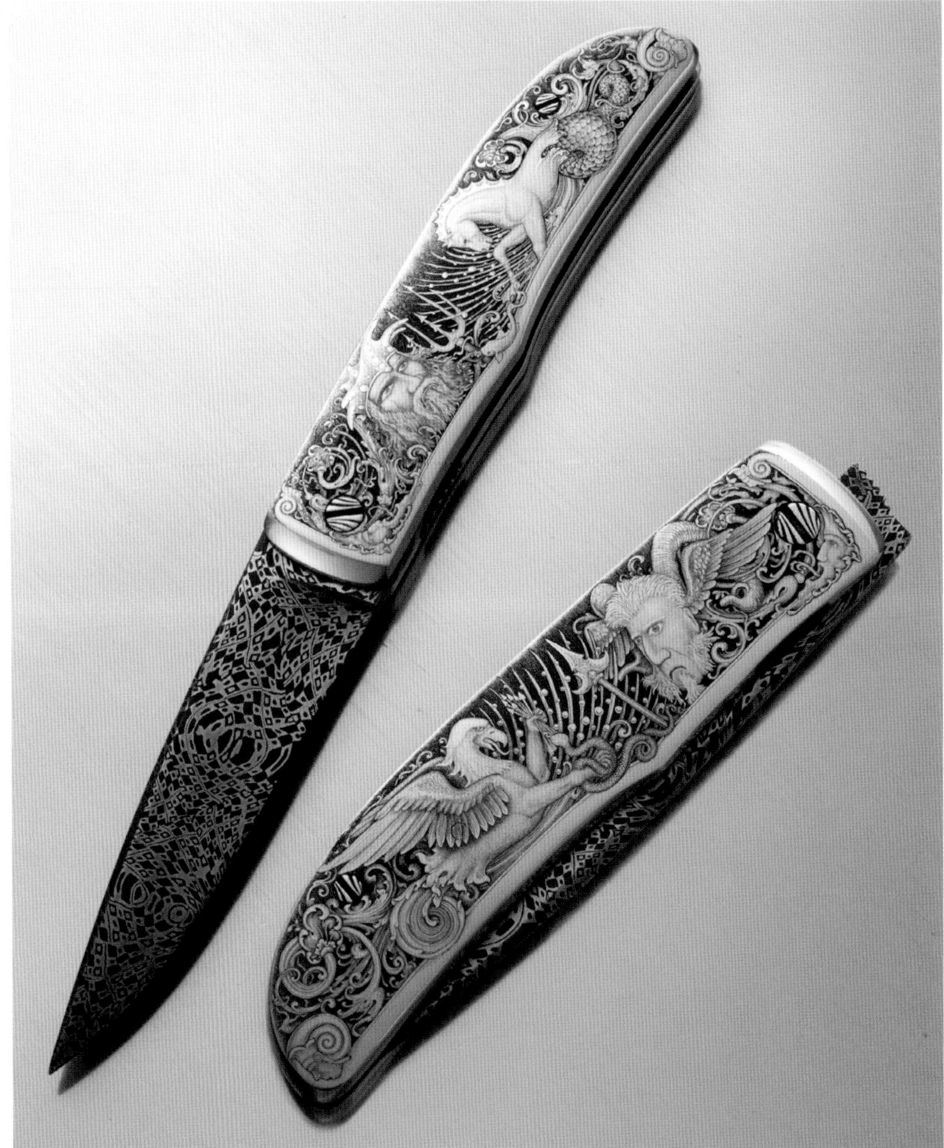

Rick Eaton

Roman Fantasy Theme Folder | 2007

OVERALL LENGTH, 6 3/4 INCHES (17.2 CM)

Mosaic high-carbon Damascus steel, stainless steel; engraved

PHOTO BY POINTSEVEN STUDIOS

Dmitriy Pavlov

Prince | 2007

OVERALL LENGTH, 8 1/16 INCHES (20.5 CM)

SAE 52100 steel, sterling silver, mammoth ivory; pierced, engraved, fabricated, carved

PHOTO BY GALINA PAVLOVA

Murad Saÿen

La Bastogne | 2005

OVERALL LENGTH, 21 1/4 INCHES (54 CM)

Damascus steel, World War II shrapnel, fossil walrus ivory, 24-karat gold, garnet; inlaid

DAMASCUS STEEL BY ROB HUDSON
PHOTO BY JIM COOPER OF SHARPBYCOOP.COM

Van Barnett

Dagger: Garden of Eden | 2001

OVERALL LENGTH, 16 1/2 INCHES (42 CM)

Ladder-pattern Damascus steel, 14-karat yellow gold, antique ivory, diamonds; forged, carved, etched, textured, inlaid, blued

PHOTO BY POINTSEVEN STUDIOS

Heather Harvey

Ribbons and Bows Dagger | 2004

OVERALL LENGTH, 11 3/4 INCHES (29.8 CM)

Mosaic Damascus steel, bell metal, 14-karat gold, fossil mammoth ivory; heat colored, cast, textured, fluted, satin finished

PHOTOS BY BLADEGALLERY.COM

Maurie McCarthy

Dagger | 2007

$15^1/_8$ X $3^{15}/_{16}$ X 1 INCHES
(38.5 X 10 X 2.5 CM)

Sterling silver, eland horn, silver wire, gold wire, diamonds; fluted, inlaid

PHOTOS BY ARTIST

George E. Dailey

Rosie | 2002

OVERALL LENGTH, 5 1/2 INCHES (14 CM)

Damascus steel, 14-karat rose gold, 14-karat white gold, diamonds, pearl

DAMASCUS STEEL BY MATTIAS STYREFORS
PHOTO BY POINTSEVEN STUDIOS

Jim Schmidt

Touch of Midas | 1994

OVERALL LENGTH, 10¼ INCHES (26 CM)

Damascus steel, black-lip pearl, 14-karat gold

PHOTO BY FRANCESCO PACHÍ

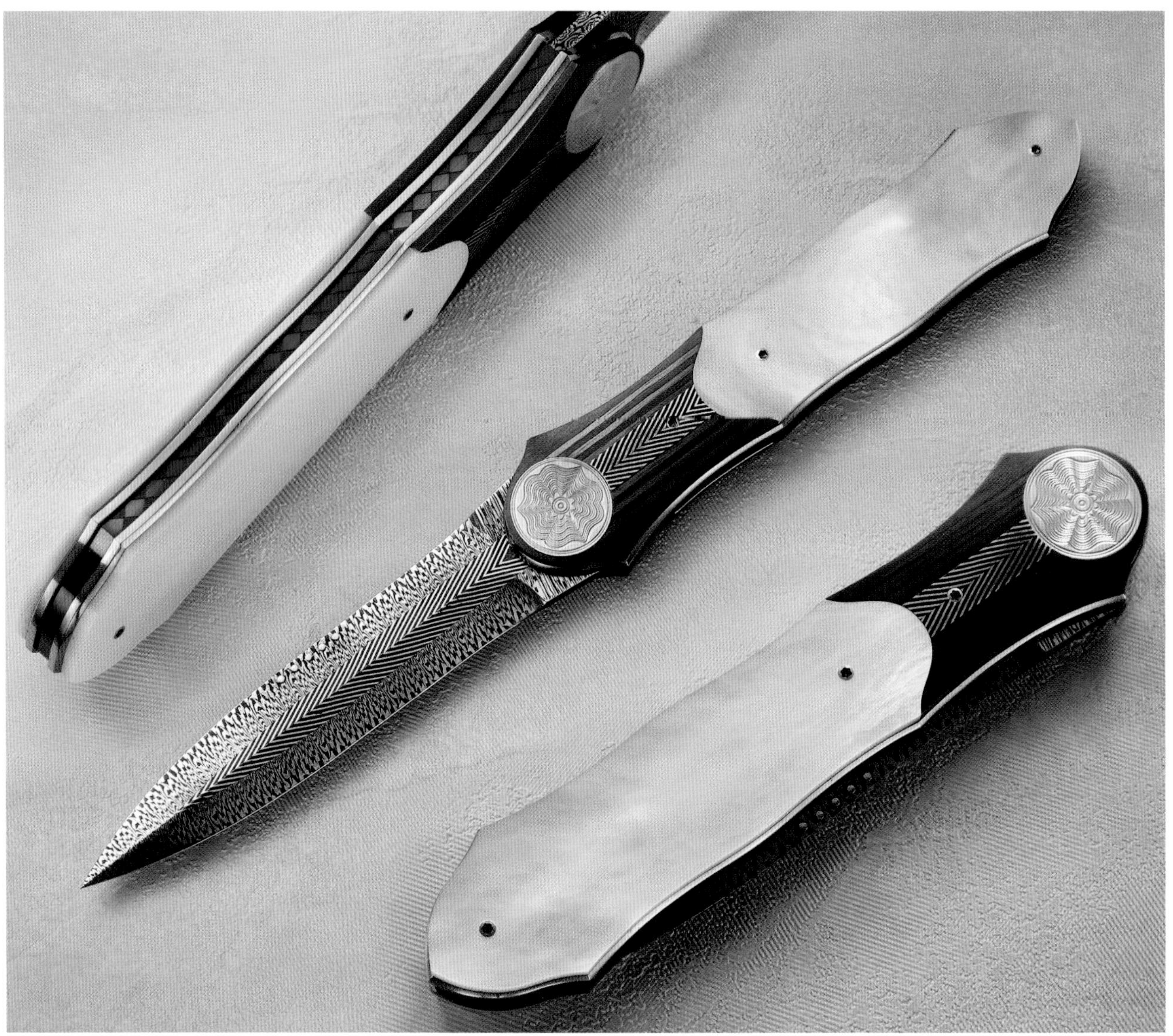

Owen Wood

Folding Boot Knife | 2006

OVERALL LENGTH, 6 3/4 INCHES (17.1 CM)

Herringbone and explosion composite Damascus steel, titanium, 303 stainless steel, gold, mother-of-pearl; decorated, blued

PHOTO BY JIM COOPER OF SHARPBYCOOP.COM

Ken Steigerwalt

English Dirk | 2004

BLADE, 4¾ INCHES (12.1 CM)

Turkish Damascus steel, nickel silver, sterling silver, checkered pearl; scalloped

DAMASCUS STEEL BY DARYL MIER
PHOTO BY JIM COOPER OF SHARPBYCOOP.COM

Stan Wilson

Balisong Number 1 | 2006

OVERALL LENGTH, 8 1/4 INCHES (21 CM)

Damascus steel, mother-of-pearl, black diamonds, 14-karat gold, 24-karat gold, titanium; file worked, jeweled, anodized

DAMASCUS STEEL BY ROBERT EGGERLING
PHOTO BY JIM COOPER OF SHARPBYCOOP.COM

Laurent Doussot

Ocean Swift | 2005

OVERALL LENGTH, 8 7/16 INCHES (21.5 CM)

Stainless Damascus steel, titanium, mother-of-pearl; carved, anodized

DAMASCUS STEEL BY DEVIN THOMAS
PHOTO BY JIM COOPER OF SHARPBYCOOP.COM

Jack Levin

Three Baroque-Style Knives | 2000

OVERALL LENGTH, 7 INCHES (17.8 CM) EACH

Swedish stainless Damascus steel, diamonds, sapphires, emeralds, 18-karat gold

PHOTO BY POINTSEVEN STUDIOS

Ron Appleton

Annabelle | 2003

OVERALL LENGTH, 7⁷⁄₈ INCHES (20 CM)

AISI-01, aluminum, bronze, titanium

PHOTO BY JIM COOPER OF SHARPBYCOOP.COM

Rick Dunkerley

Untitled | 2007

Mosaic Damascus steel, 18-karat gold, 24-karat gold, diamond; inlaid, file worked, nitre blued, set

PHOTO BY POINTSEVEN STUDIOS

Johnny Stout

The Raptor | 2007

OVERALL LENGTH, 7¾ INCHES (19.7 CM)

Explosion-pattern Damascus steel, mosaic bolsters, mammoth ivory, gold, copper; engraved

DAMASCUS STEEL BY MATTIAS STYREFORS
ENGRAVED BY JIM SMALL
BOLSTERS BY ROBERT EGGERLING
PHOTO BY JIM COOPER OF SHARPBYCOOP.COM

Donald J. Vogt

Autumn Bloom | 2005

8$\frac{1}{2}$ X 1$\frac{1}{16}$ X $\frac{7}{16}$ INCHES (21.6 X 2.7 X 1.1 CM)

Damascus steel, 440C stainless steel, 14-karat gold, ruby, black-lip pearl, titanium; ground, carved, heat-treated, embellished, mounted, engraved, profiled, acid etched, hardened, hammered, file worked, color anodized

PHOTO BY POINTSEVEN STUDIOS

Alistair Bastian

Picture-Frame Folder | 2006

8 X 1 X 3/8 INCHES (20 X 2.5 X 1 CM)

Mosaic Damascus steel, stainless steel; hand carved

PHOTO BY ARTIST

Richard Steven Wright

Ambidextrous Bolster-Release Switchblade Dagger | 2007

OVERALL LENGTH, 9 9/16 INCHES (24.3 CM);
BLADE, 4 3/8 INCHES (11.1 CM)

Turkish-twist Damascus steel, titanium, lapis lazuli, enamel; forged, hollow ground, treated, relieved, carved

TURKISH-TWIST DAMASCUS STEEL BY JERRY RADOS
PHOTOS BY ARTIST

Ty Montell

Silver-Inlay Skinner | 2007

OVERALL LENGTH, 9 1/4 INCHES (23.5 CM)

440C stainless steel, nickel silver, white silver, water buffalo horn, sterling silver; hollow ground, mirror polished, inlaid

PHOTO BY TERRILL HOFFMAN

Michael Miller

Apple Blossom Bowie | 2007

1 3/16 X 10 13/16 X 1 9/16 INCHES (3 X 27.5 X 4 CM)

Damascus steel, carbon-nickel steels, juniper burl, iron, malachite; inlaid, forge welded

PHOTOS BY JOE OFRIA

Roger Bergh

Cone | 2005

OVERALL LENGTH, 6 11/16 INCHES (17 CM)

Mosaic and firecracker-pattern Damascus steel, warthog tusk, sallow burl; carved

PHOTO BY JIM COOPER OF SHARPBYCOOP.COM

E. Jay Hendrickson

Classic Clip-Point Bowie

OVERALL LENGTH, 17 INCHES (43.2 CM)

Fine silver, curly maple; inlaid, carved

PHOTO BY JIM COOPER OF SHARPBYCOOP.COM

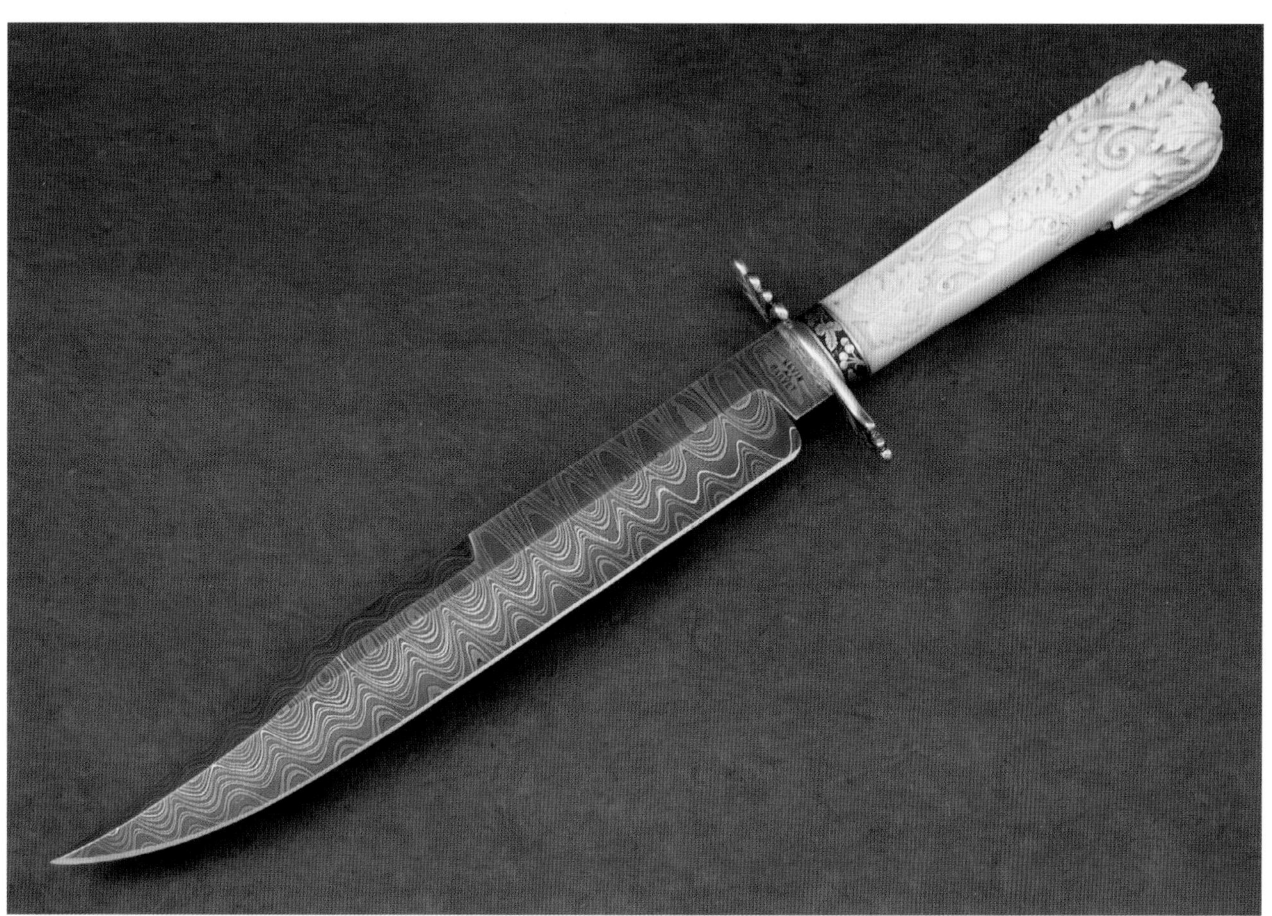

Kevin Harvey

Fruits of the Vine | 2005

OVERALL LENGTH, 14 1/8 INCHES (35.9 CM)

Ladder- and flash-pattern Damascus steel, hippopotamus tooth, nickel silver, dark pango wood; forged, hand carved, engraved, sculpted, inlaid

FORGED BY HEATHER HARVEY
PHOTO BY BLADEGALLERY.COM

Allen Elishewitz

Scarab Fixed Blade | 2007

$1^{3}/_{8}$ X $13^{3}/_{8}$ X $^{3}/_{4}$ INCHES (3.5 X 34 X 2 CM)

Stainless Damascus steel, paper Micarta, stainless steel; machine cut, hand ground

PHOTO BY VALERIE ELISHEWITZ

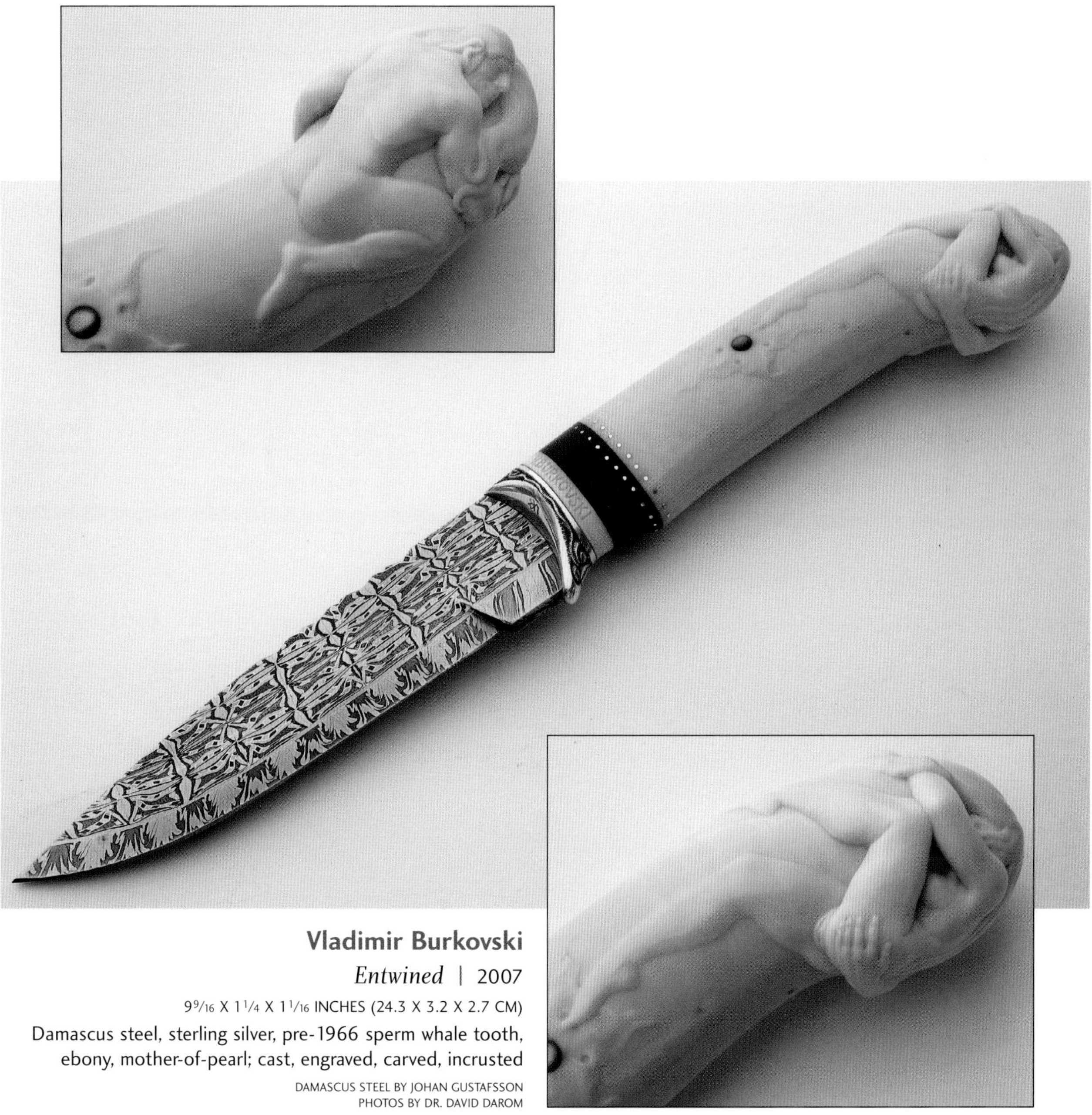

Vladimir Burkovski

Entwined | 2007

$9^{9}/_{16}$ X $1^{1}/_{4}$ X $1^{1}/_{16}$ INCHES (24.3 X 3.2 X 2.7 CM)

Damascus steel, sterling silver, pre-1966 sperm whale tooth, ebony, mother-of-pearl; cast, engraved, carved, incrusted

DAMASCUS STEEL BY JOHAN GUSTAFSSON
PHOTOS BY DR. DAVID DAROM

Mitch Edwards

Gentleman's Bowie | 2007

OVERALL LENGTH, 10 INCHES (25.4 CM)

Damascus steel, ivory; blued

PHOTO BY JIM COOPER OF SHARPBYCOOP.COM

John Horrigan

The Texan | 2005

OVERALL LENGTH, 16 1/8 INCHES (41 CM)

Ladder-pattern Damascus steel, elephant ivory, steel; blued, fluted

PHOTO BY STEVE WOODS

Dan Graves

D-Guard Short Saber | 2007

21 1/2 X 4 1/2 X 9/16 INCHES (54.6 X 11.4 X 1.5 CM)

Damascus steel, African blackwood; hand forged

PHOTO BY JIM COOPER OF SHARPBYCOOP.COM

Anders Högström

Hanson and Högström San Fran Dagger | 2008

BLADE, 11 13/16 INCHES (30 CM)

Hanson Damascus steel, sterling silver, fossil walrus

PHOTO BY JIM COOPER OF SHARPBYCOOP.COM

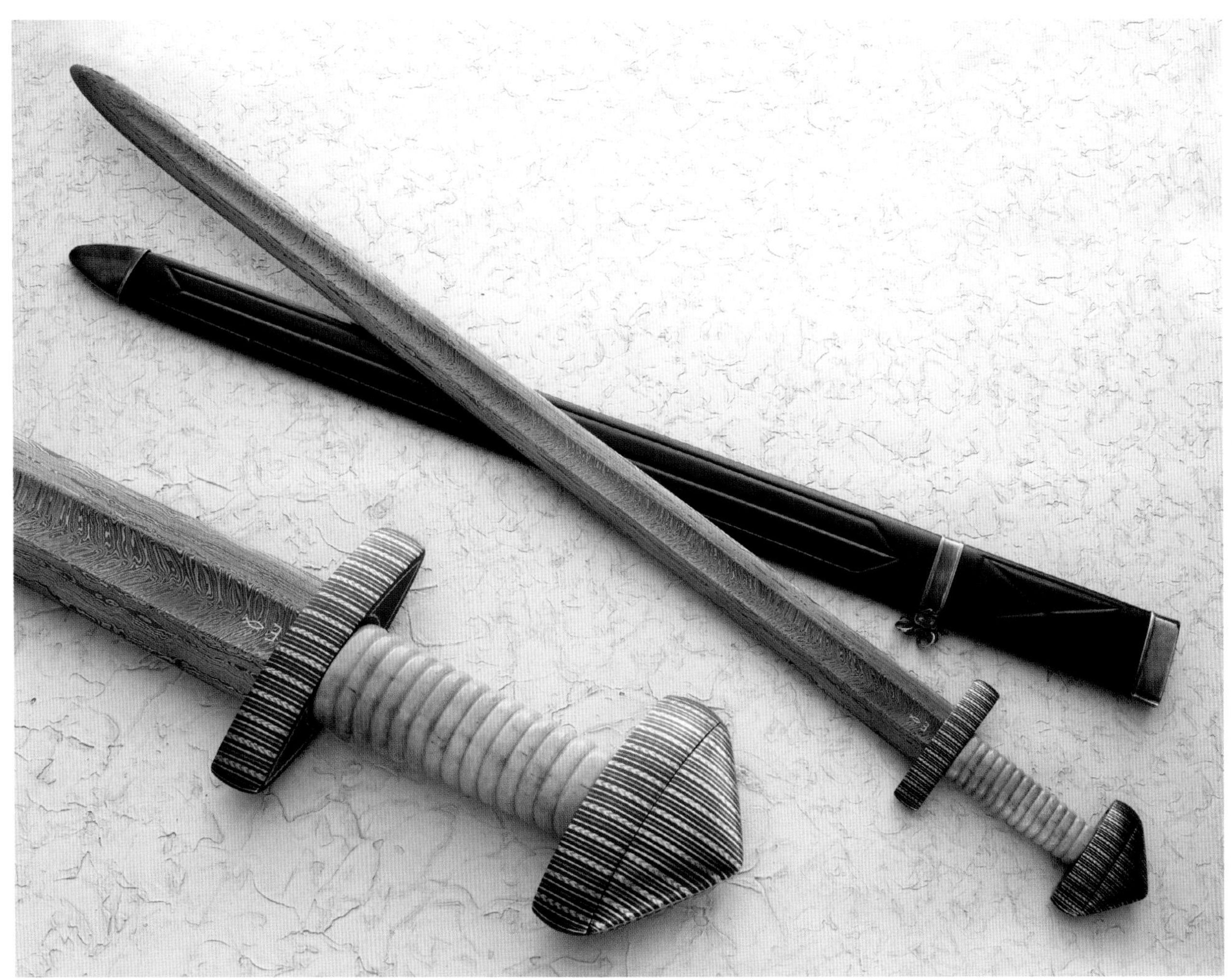

Vince Evans

Viking Sword | 2006

OVERALL LENGTH, $37^{3}/_{8}$ INCHES (95 CM)

Damascus steel, copper and silver wire, bone; blued, welded, inlaid

PHOTO BY POINTSEVEN STUDIOS

Bailey Bradshaw

Persian Integral Camp Set | 2006

OVERALL LENGTH, 16 INCHES (40.6 CM)

Damascus steel, 22-karat gold wire, snakewood; inlaid

PHOTO BY JIM COOPER OF SHARPBYCOOP.COM

J.D. Smith

Black Dagger | 2007

OVERALL LENGTH, 15 INCHES (38.1 CM)

15N20 steel, 1084 steel, African blackwood; pattern welded, carved

PHOTO BY JIM COOPER OF SHARPBYCOOP.COM

Bill McHenry

Pogue Mahone | 1989

OVERALL LENGTH, 7⁷⁄₈ INCHES (20 CM)

Damascus steel, Siberian impala, silver; engraved

PHOTO BY JIM COOPER OF SHARPBYCOOP.COM

Dan Graves

Gentleman's Presentation Fighter | 2007

14½ X ¾ X ¾ INCHES (36.8 X 1.9 X 2 CM)

Damascus steel, elephant ivory; hand forged

PHOTO BY JIM COOPER OF SHARPBYCOOP.COM

Dan Gray

Belly of the Beast | 2007

OVERALL LENGTH, 12 INCHES (30.5 CM)

01 steel, water buffalo horn, rubies, black-tail rattlesnake

SHEATH BY DAN GRAY
PHOTO BY JIM COOPER OF SHARPBYCOOP.COM

Dan Graves

Quillon Dagger | 2007

16½ X 4½ X 1 INCHES
(41.9 X 11.4 X 2.5 CM)

Damascus steel, nickel silver, sterling silver, elephant ivory; hand forged

PHOTO BY JIM COOPER OF SHARPBYCOOP.COM

Kevin Harvey

Ladder and Flash Quillon Dagger | 2003

OVERALL LENGTH, 16¾ INCHES (42.5 CM)

Ladder- and flash-pattern Damascus steel, bronze, nickel silver, African blackwood, silver wire, brass wire, warthog tooth bead; forged, fluted, twisted

PHOTO BY BLADEGALLERY.COM

Raymond B. Rybar, Jr.
Tribute to Bill Moran, the Master of Damascus | 2006
16 X 3 X 1 INCHES (40.6 X 7.6 X 2.5 CM)
High-carbon steel, nickel 200, silver, curly maple; forged
PHOTO BY POINTSEVEN STUDIOS

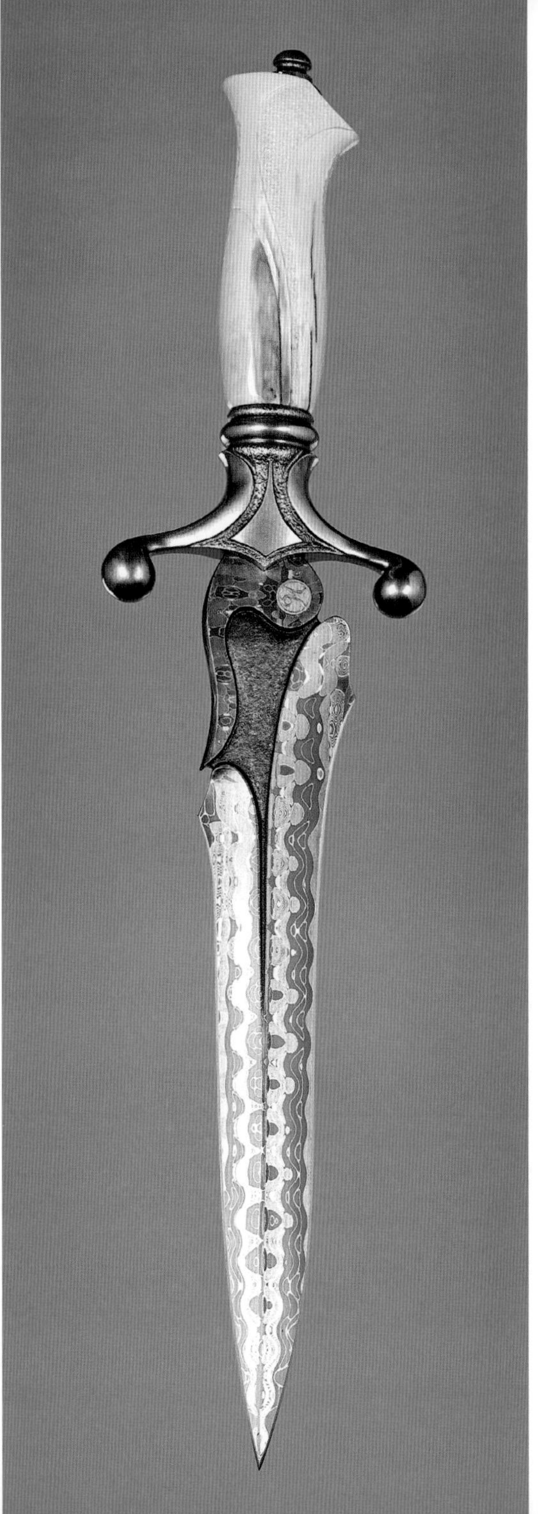

Peter Mason

Walrus Fighter | 2007

14 9/16 X 4 11/16 X 12 9/16 INCHES (37 X 12 X 32 CM)

Mosaic Damascus steel, bronze, walrus ivory

BLADE BY ETTORÉ GIANFERRARI
PHOTO BY DORIAN SPENCE

Tommy McNabb

Twin Peaks | 2006

LONGEST OVERALL LENGTH, $8\frac{1}{2}$ INCHES (21.6 CM)

Stainless Damascus steel, turquoise, amber, wood, silver; forged, ground, etched

PHOTO BY MCNABB STUDIO, INC.

Schuyler Lovestrand

Model H-8 Drop-Point Hunter | 1987

OVERALL LENGTH, 8¼ INCHES (21 CM)

ATS-34 steel, 416 stainless steel, mammoth ivory

PHOTO BY JIM COOPER OF SHARPBYCOOP.COM

Salvatore Puddu

Watch-Pocket Folder | 2005

OVERALL LENGTH, 4 5/8 INCHES (11.8 CM)

Ancient tortoiseshell, gold; inlaid

PHOTO BY FRANCESCO PACHÍ

J.A. Harkins

Maxim | 2008

OVERALL LENGTH, 7 7/8 INCHES (20 CM)

416 stainless steel, CPM S30V steel

PHOTO BY JIM COOPER OF SHARPBYCOOP.COM

Antonio Fogarizzu

Small Folding Dagger | 2006

OVERALL LENGTH, 6 5/16 INCHES (16 CM)

RWL 34 steel, 416 stainless steel, ancient tortoiseshell

PHOTO BY JIM COOPER OF SHARPBYCOOP.COM

Gail Lunn

Black Gold | 2007

OVERALL LENGTH, 24 3/8 INCHES (61.9 CM)

Damascus steel, tortoiseshell, gold nugget button, gold nugget thumbstud; file worked

PHOTO BY JIM COOPER OF SHARPBYCOOP.COM

Brent Sandow

Nordic Hunter | 2007

$1\frac{3}{16}$ X $\frac{3}{8}$ X $9\frac{1}{16}$ INCHES (3 X 1 X 23 CM)

Turkish Damascus steel, mammoth ivory; tang constructed

PHOTO BY NORMAN SANDOW

Kaj Embretsen

Back-Lock Inter-Frame Folder

Explosion Damascus steel, sambar stag, gold; inlaid

PHOTO BY JIM COOPER OF SHARPBYCOOP.COM

Steven R. Johnson
Loveless-Style Slab-Hilt Fighter | 2007
OVERALL LENGTH, 11 3/8 INCHES (29 CM)
154CM steel, 416 stainless steel, sambar stag
PHOTO BY POINTSEVEN STUDIOS

Curt Erickson

Art Dagger | 2007

BLADE, 9 1/2 INCHES (24.1 CM)

440C stainless steel, dendrite agate, gold, platinum; engraved

ENGRAVED BY JULIE WARENSKI-ERICKSON
PHOTO BY JIM COOPER OF SHARPBYCOOP.COM

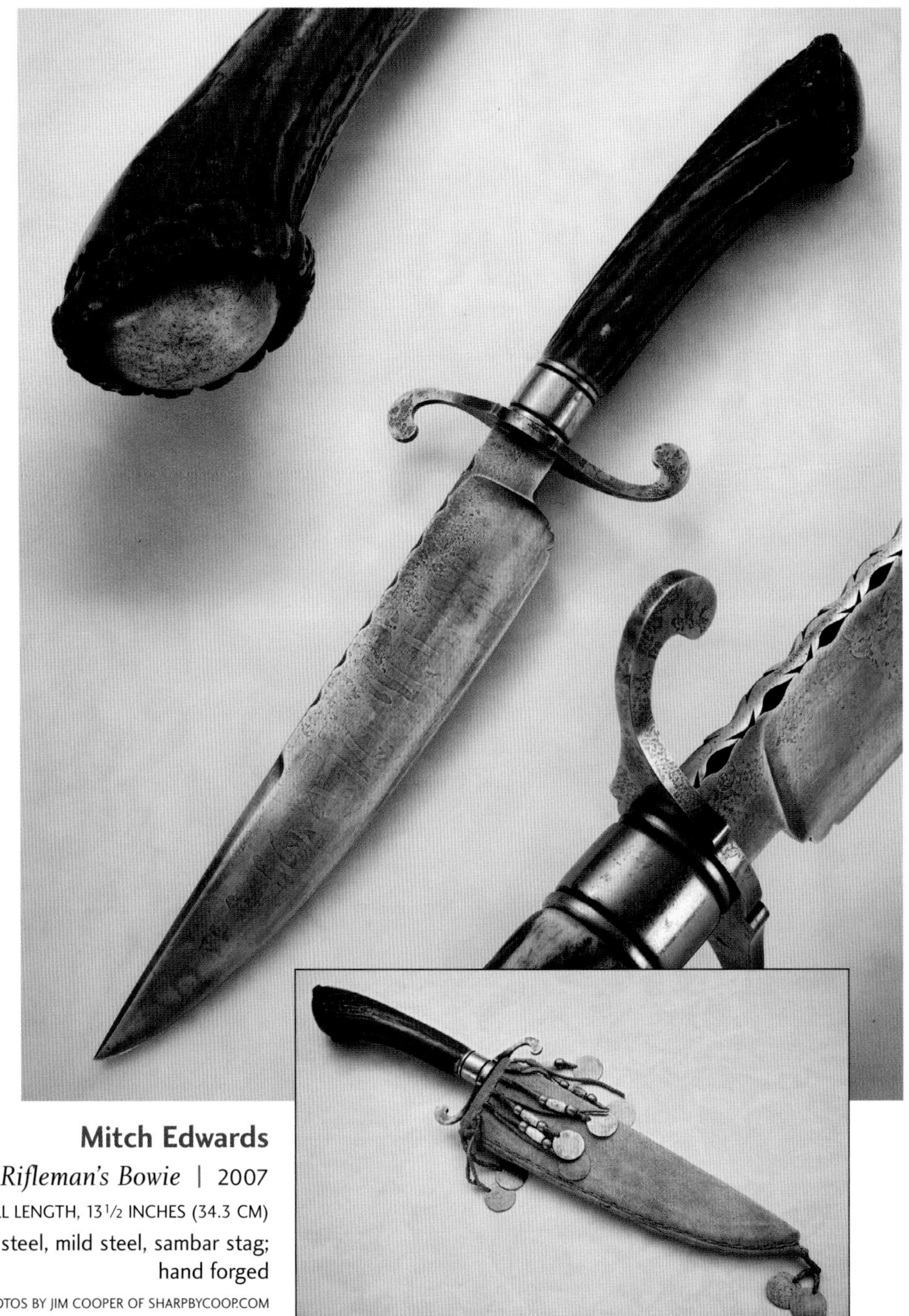

Mitch Edwards

Rifleman's Bowie | 2007

OVERALL LENGTH, 13 1/2 INCHES (34.3 CM)

1065 steel, mild steel, sambar stag; hand forged

PHOTOS BY JIM COOPER OF SHARPBYCOOP.COM

Daniel Winkler

Lost Lake Camp Knife | 2007

OVERALL LENGTH, 10 7/8 INCHES (27.6 CM)

Random Damascus steel, elk antler, copper

PHOTO BY JIM COOPER OF SHARPBYCOOP.COM

Anders Högström

Invalidator Bowie | 2008

OVERALL LENGTH, 17 11/16 INCHES (45 CM)

1050 carbon steel, sterling silver, walrus ivory, leather; clay tempered, antiqued, textured

PHOTO BY JIM COOPER OF SHARPBYCOOP.COM

Mace Vitale

Rib Tickler | 2007

OVERALL LENGTH, 17½ INCHES (45 CM)

1075 steel, nickel silver, copper, curly maple; hand forged

PHOTO BY JIM COOPER OF SHARPBYCOOP.COM

Thinus Herbst

Fighting Knife | 2007

20⅞ X 2¾ X 1 INCHES (53 X 7 X 2.5 CM)

12C27 stainless steel, Damascus steel, desert ironwood, titanium; hand filed, bead blasted

PHOTO BY DEWALD REINERS

Roger Bergh

Dark Player | 2004

OVERALL LENGTH, 7⁷⁄₈ INCHES (20 CM)

Checkerboard- and firecracker-pattern Damascus steel, birch burl, ebony, mammoth ivory

PHOTO BY JIM COOPER OF SHARPBYCOOP.COM

Stephen Mackrill, Sr.

Death Before Dishonor Californian Bowie | 2006

$10^{1}/_{4}$ X 8 X $^{1}/_{16}$ INCHES (25.9 X 20.3 X 0.4 CM)

Stainless Damascus steel, silver, brass, lapis lazuli; engraved

ENGRAVED BY BARRY LEE HANDS
DAMASCUS STEEL BY HEATHER HARVEY
PHOTO BY POINTSEVEN STUDIOS

E. Jay Hendrickson

Clip-Point Bowie | 2006

OVERALL LENGTH, 15 INCHES (38.1 CM);
BLADE, 10 INCHES (25.4 CM)

5160 steel, curly maple, fine silver, nickel silver; inlaid, wrapped, file worked, rounded, carved, peened

PHOTO BY POINTSEVEN STUDIOS

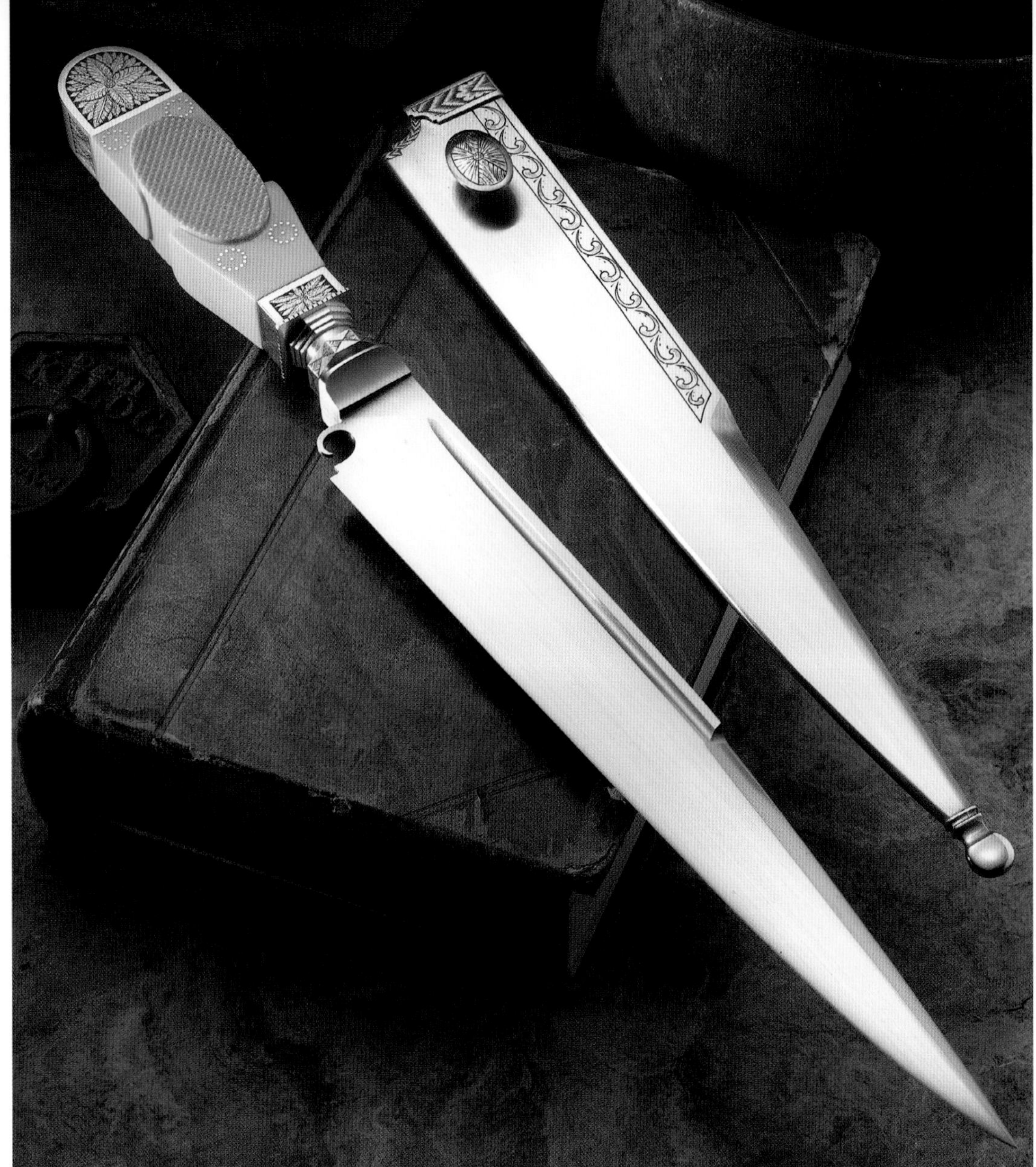

Harvey Dean

Samuel Bell Bowie Reproduction, Circa 1850s | 2006

OVERALL LENGTH, 13 1/4 INCHES (33.7 CM)

01 steel, sterling silver, ivory, nickel silver; forged, engraved

ENGRAVED BY STEVE DUNN
PHOTO BY STEVE WOODS

Stephen Mackrill, Sr.

Big-Bear Fighting Knife | 2005

8 1/4 X 10 X 1/16 INCHES (20.8 X 25.4 X 0.4 CM)

Stainless chromium steel, leadwood, hippopotamus tooth, silver; mirror polished, inlaid

PHOTO BY POINTSEVEN STUDIOS

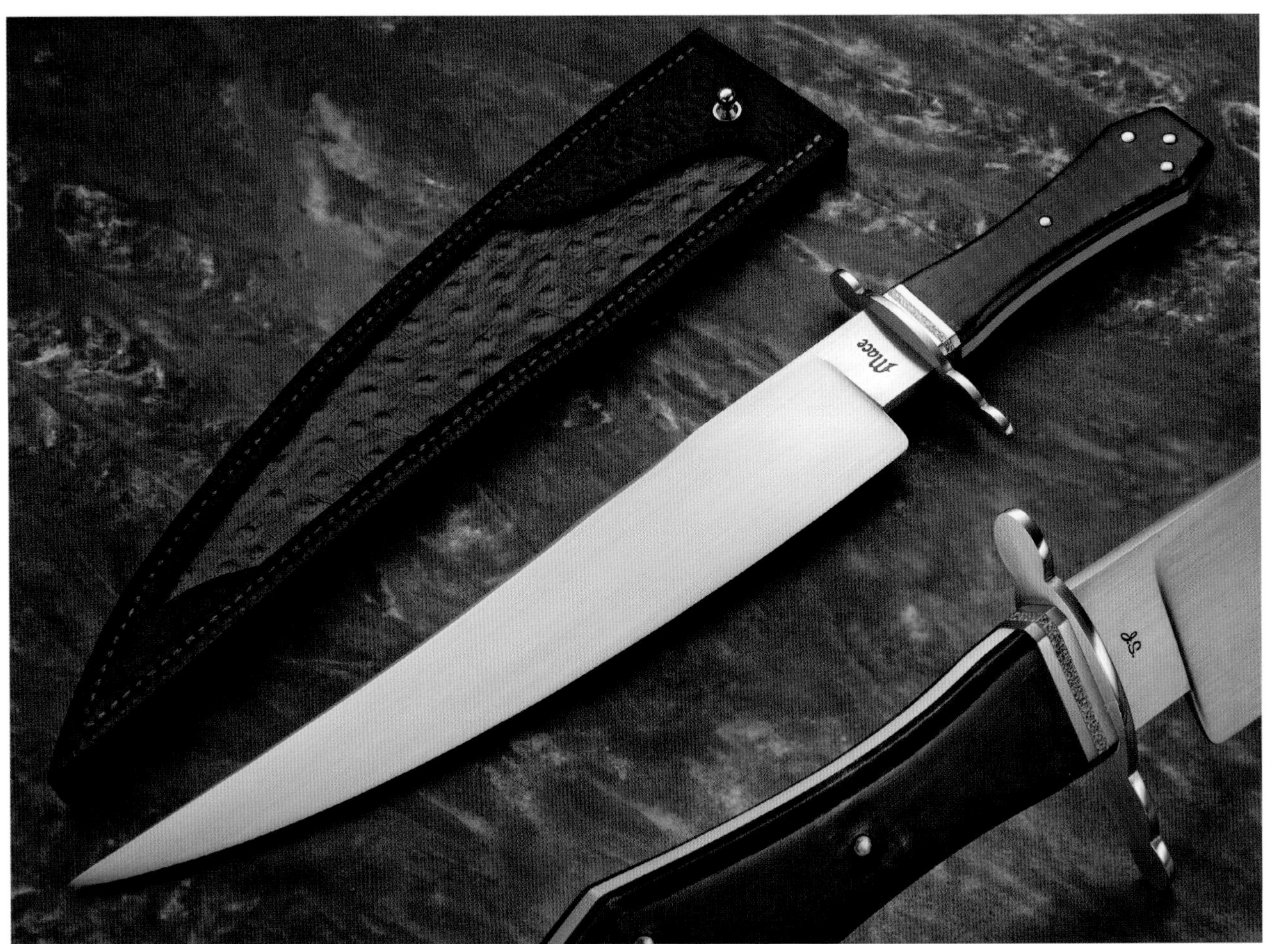

Mace Vitale

Point Breeze Bowie | 2007

OVERALL LENGTH, 18$\frac{1}{2}$ INCHES (47.5 CM)

1095 steel, nickel silver, copper, curly maple; hand forged

PHOTO BY JIM COOPER OF SHARPBYCOOP.COM

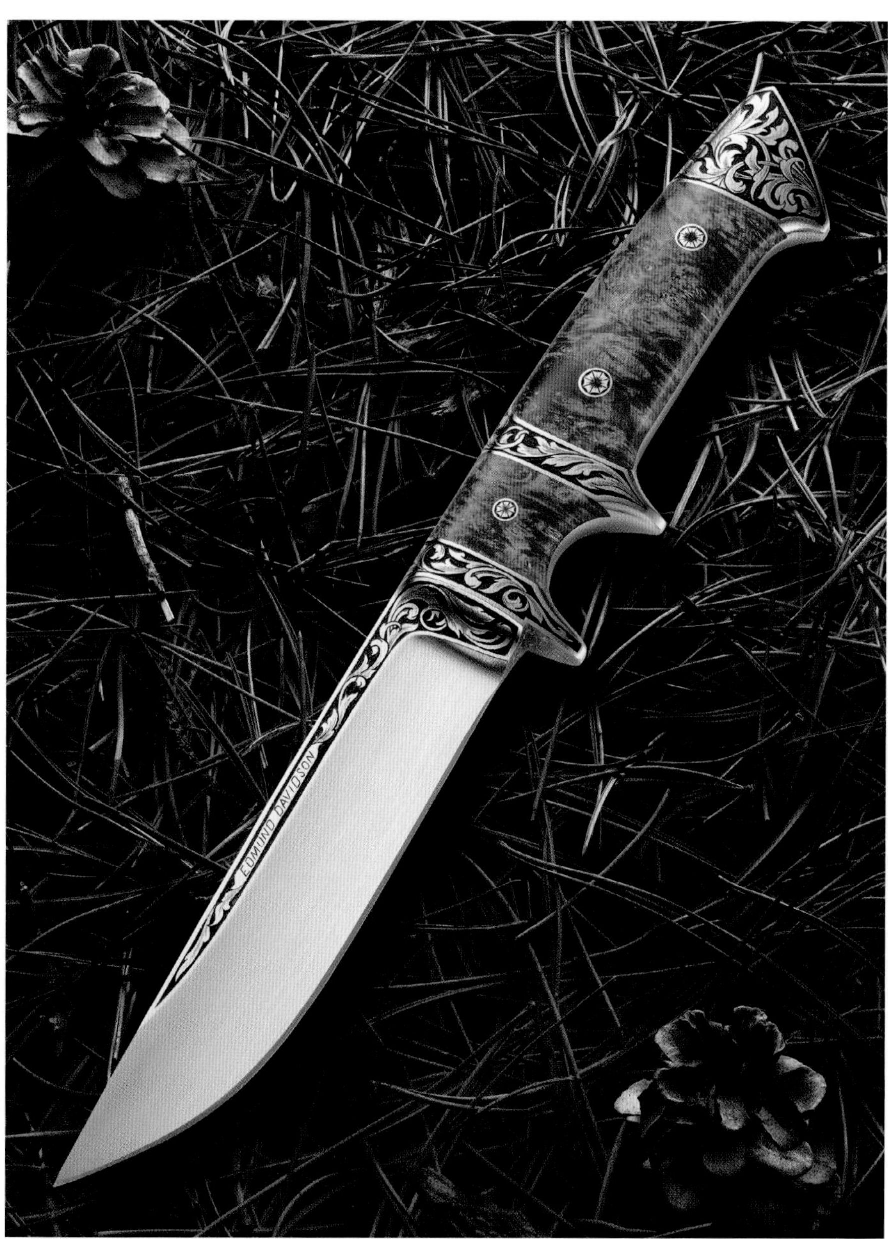

Edmund Davidson

David Darom Sub-Hilt | 2006

OVERALL LENGTH, $10\frac{1}{8}$ INCHES (25.7 CM)

440C stainless steel, box elder; engraved, heat-treated, integral constructed

ENGRAVED BY JERE DAVIDSON
HEAT-TREATED BY PAUL BOS
PHOTO BY POINTSEVEN STUDIOS

Dmitriy Pavlov

Steppe | 2006

OVERALL LENGTH, 12³⁄₈ INCHES (31.5 CM)

Damascus steel, sterling silver, purpleheart; forged, fabricated, engraved

PHOTO BY GALINA PAVLOVA

David Lang

Horse-Head Bowie | 2005

$16\frac{1}{2}$ X $2\frac{9}{16}$ X $1\frac{3}{16}$ INCHES (42 X 6.5 X 3 CM)

440C stainless steel, desert ironwood burl, silver

PHOTO BY POINTSEVEN STUDIOS

Edmund Davidson

Gordon's Push Dagger | 1999

OVERALL LENGTH, 8 1/4 INCHES (21 CM)

A-2 steel, ivory; hollow ground, engraved, heat-treated, scrimshawed, integral constructed

ENGRAVED BY JERE DAVIDSON
HEAT-TREATED BY PAUL BOS
SCRIMSHAWED BY LINDA KARST STONE
PHOTO BY POINTSEVEN STUDIOS

Richard Sexstone

Upwind Downwind | 2007

OVERALL LENGTH, 8 INCHES (20.3 CM)

Damascus steel, 203E steel, pure iron Damascus steel; die formed, engraved

PHOTO BY JIM COOPER OF SHARPBYCOOP.COM

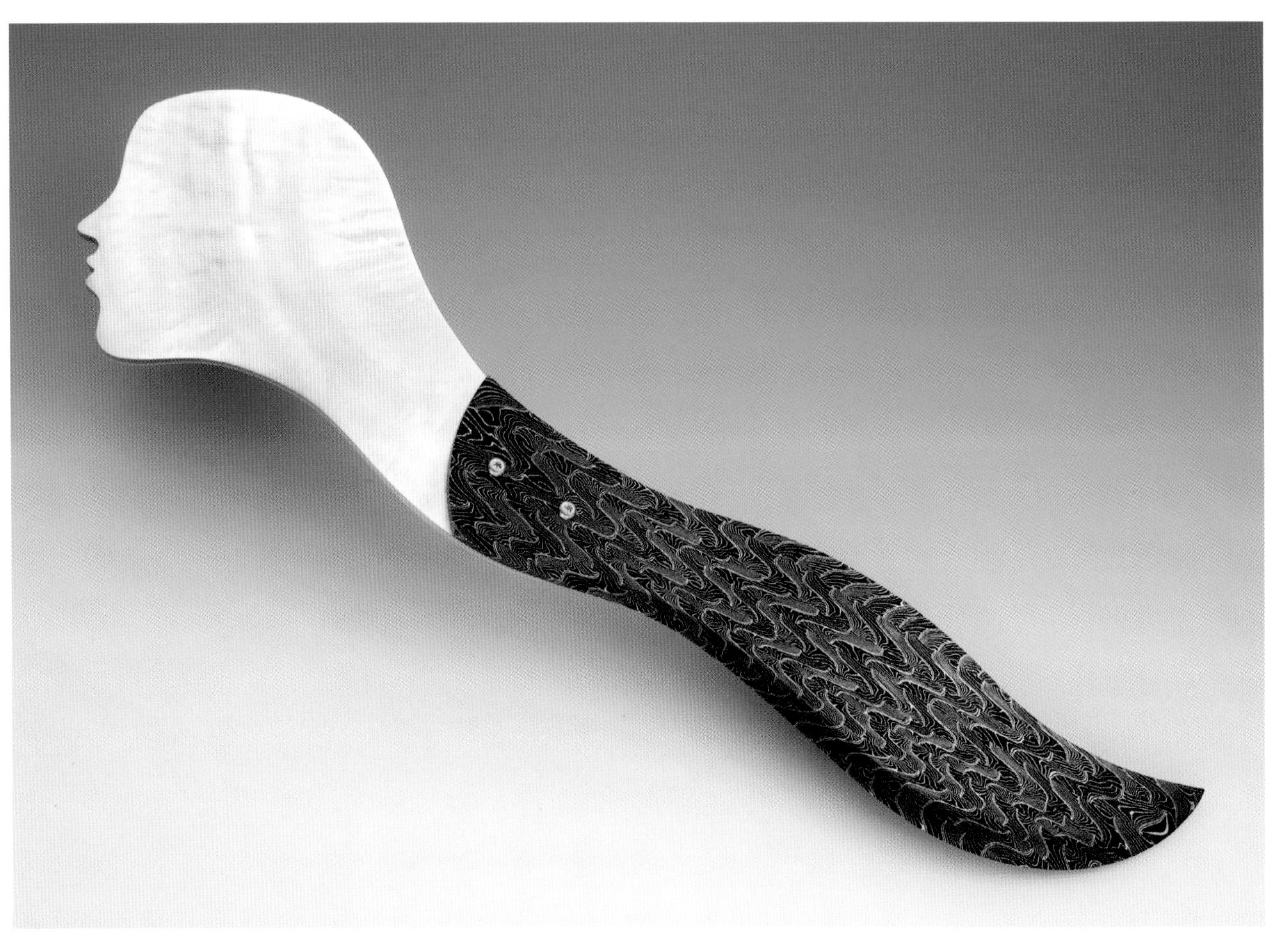

Jeffrey Cornwell

Pearl Diver | 2007

11 X 1 X 1/4 INCHES (28 X 2.5 X 0.6 CM)

O-1 steel, gold-lip mother-of-pearl; etched, heat colored

PHOTO BY JIM COOPER OF SHARPBYCOOP.COM

Tadashi Koizumi

A la Geoff Riggle Number 1 | 2007

1 X 1 X 1 INCHES (2.5 X 2.5 X 2.5 CM)

Bronze; cast

PHOTO BY JEFF SABO

Phil Carrizzi
David Cronin
Strato | 2007
$10^{1}/_{4}$ X $2^{3}/_{8}$ X $2^{3}/_{8}$ INCHES
(26 X 6 X 6 CM)
Damascus steel;
polychromed, fused
PHOTO BY DOUG YAPLE

Jeffrey Cornwell

Peacock | 2008

13 1/8 X 1 9/16 X 1/4 INCHES
(33.4 X 4 X 0.7 CM)

Random Damascus steel; etched, polished

DAMASCUS STEEL BY ROBERT EGGERLING
PHOTO BY JIM COOPER OF SHARPBYCOOP.COM

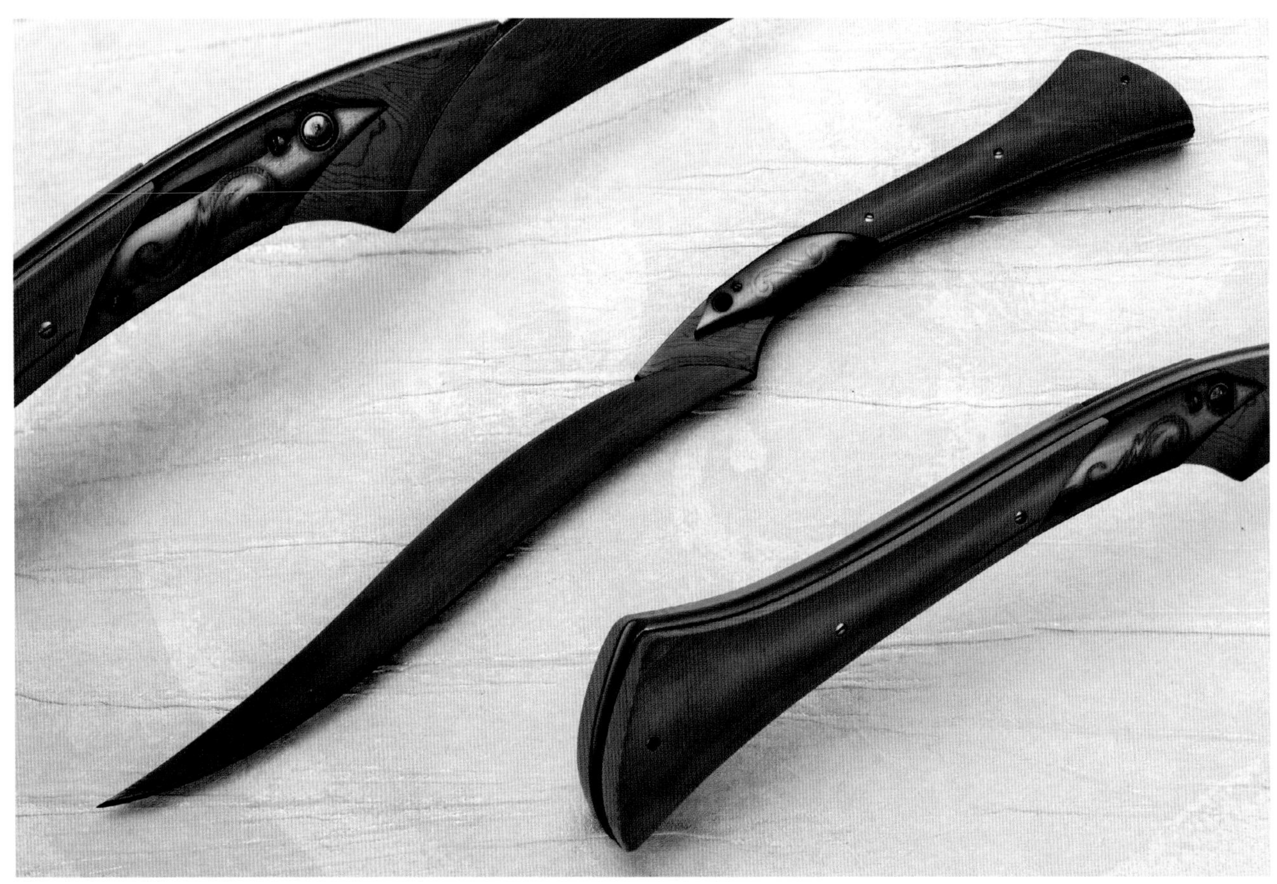

Bertie Rietveld

Panache | 2001

OVERALL LENGTH, 10 7/16 INCHES (26.5 CM)

Colored stainless Damascus steel, stainless steel, 24-karat gold, caramel mammoth ivory; inlaid

PHOTO BY JIM COOPER OF SHARPBYCOOP.COM

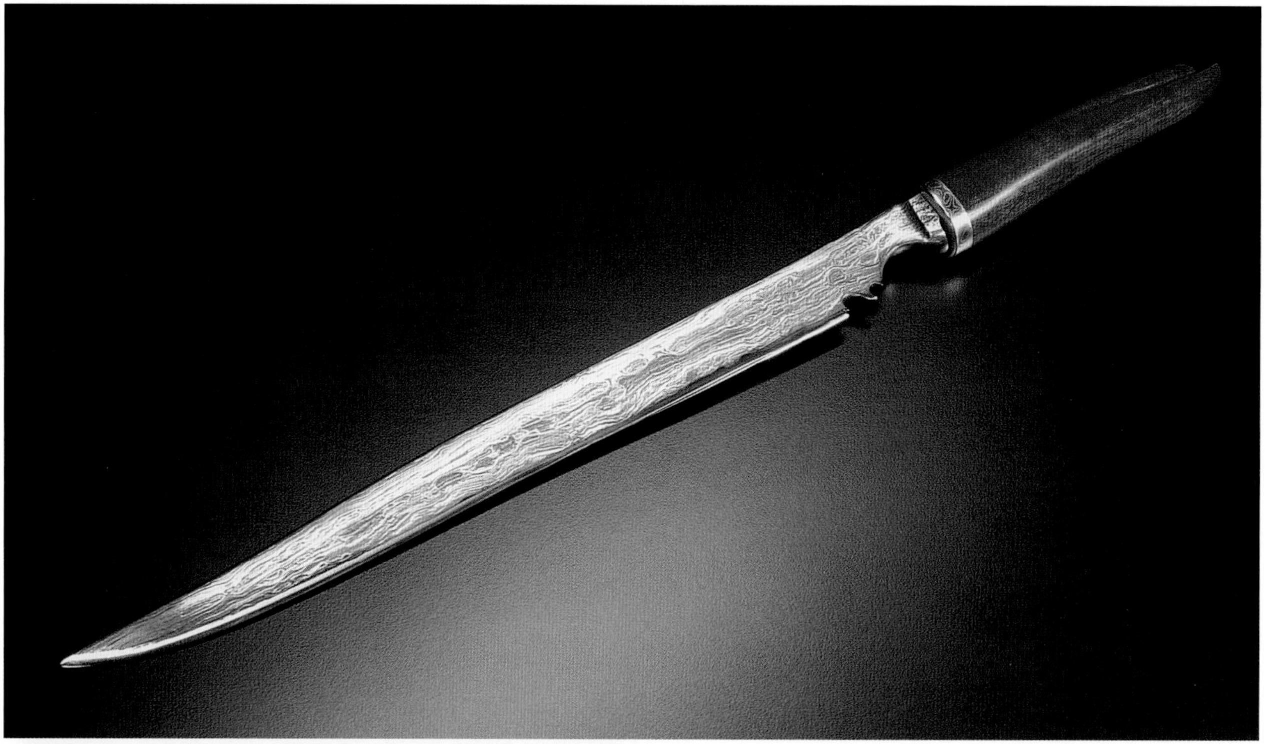

Robert Coogan

French Tickler | 2007

1 X 17 5/16 X 3/4 INCHES (2.5 X 44 X 2 CM)

Steel, mokume gane, purpleheart; laminated, forged, fabricated, carved

PHOTOS BY TTU PHOTO SERVICES

Mardi Meshejian

Drill-Rod Dagger | 2004

OVERALL LENGTH, 13 INCHES (33 CM)

Drill-rod Damascus steel, copper, walrus ivory; cast

PHOTO BY JIM COOPER OF SHARPBYCOOP.COM

Johnny Stout

The Zodiac | 2007

15/16 X 9/16 X 7 11/16 INCHES (2.4 X 1.4 X 19.5 CM)

Paisley Damascus steel, bark mammoth ivory; engraved

DAMASCUS STEEL BY ROBERT EGGERLING
ENGRAVED BY JOE MASON
PHOTO BY JIM COOPER OF SHARPBYCOOP.COM

Vince Evans

Turkish Yataghan | 2007

OVERALL LENGTH, 25 3/16 INCHES (64 CM)

Turkish-ribbon Damascus steel, silver, fossil ivory; engraved

PHOTO BY POINTSEVEN STUDIOS

Tim Hancock

Dog-Bone Dagger #1 | 2005

OVERALL LENGTH, 12 9/16 INCHES (32 CM)

Damascus steel, ancient walrus ivory; hand made

PHOTO BY JIM COOPER OF SHARPBYCOOP.COM

Jody Muller

Untitled | 2007

OVERALL LENGTH, 7 1/16 INCHES (18 CM)

Damascus steel, green mammoth ivory, 24-karat gold; inlaid, blued, sculpted, hand engraved

PHOTO BY JIM COOPER OF SHARPBYCOOP.COM

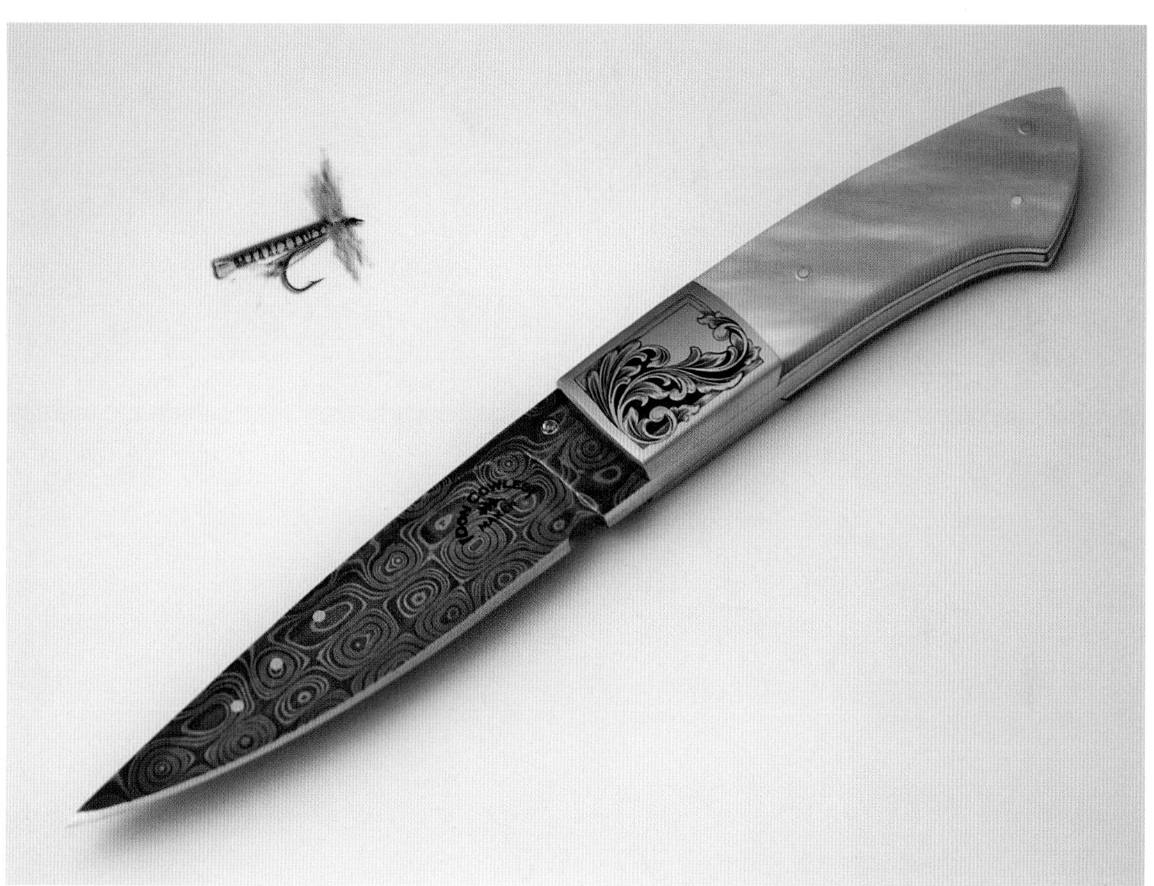

Don Cowles

Gold-Lip Spear | 2005

OVERALL LENGTH, 5 1/2 INCHES (14 CM)

Raindrop-pattern Damascus steel, 416 stainless steel, 14-karat gold, gold-lip mother-of-pearl, topaz; set, hand engraved, inlaid

ENGRAVED AND INLAID BY JIM SMALL
PHOTO BY ARTIST

Kaj Embretsen

Drop-Point Back-Lock Folder | 2008

Damascus steel, mammoth ivory, nickel Damascus, gold

PHOTO BY JIM COOPER OF SHARPBYCOOP.COM

Gerald E. Corbit

Large Model 9 | 2004

OVERALL LENGTH, 7 INCHES (17.8 CM)

Mosaic Damascus steel, mother-of-pearl, 14-karat gold, 24-karat gold; engraved, inlaid

DAMASCUS STEEL BY ROBERT EGGERLING
ENGRAVED BY BRUCE SHAW
PHOTO BY JIM COOPER OF SHARPBYCOOP.COM

Norman E. Sandow

The Ellops | 2007

$9\frac{13}{16}$ X $\frac{1}{2}$ X $1\frac{3}{16}$ INCHES (25 X 1.3 X 3 CM)

ATS-34 steel, titanium, ivory, gold pins;
mirror polished, file worked, jeweled

PHOTO BY ARTIST

Howard Hitchmough

Iridescence | 2005

OVERALL LENGTH, 7 11/16 INCHES (19.5 CM)

Stainless Damascus steel, carbon Damascus, white pearl, 18-karat gold, garnet, 24-karat gold, titanium; twisted, blued

PHOTO BY POINTSEVEN STUDIOS

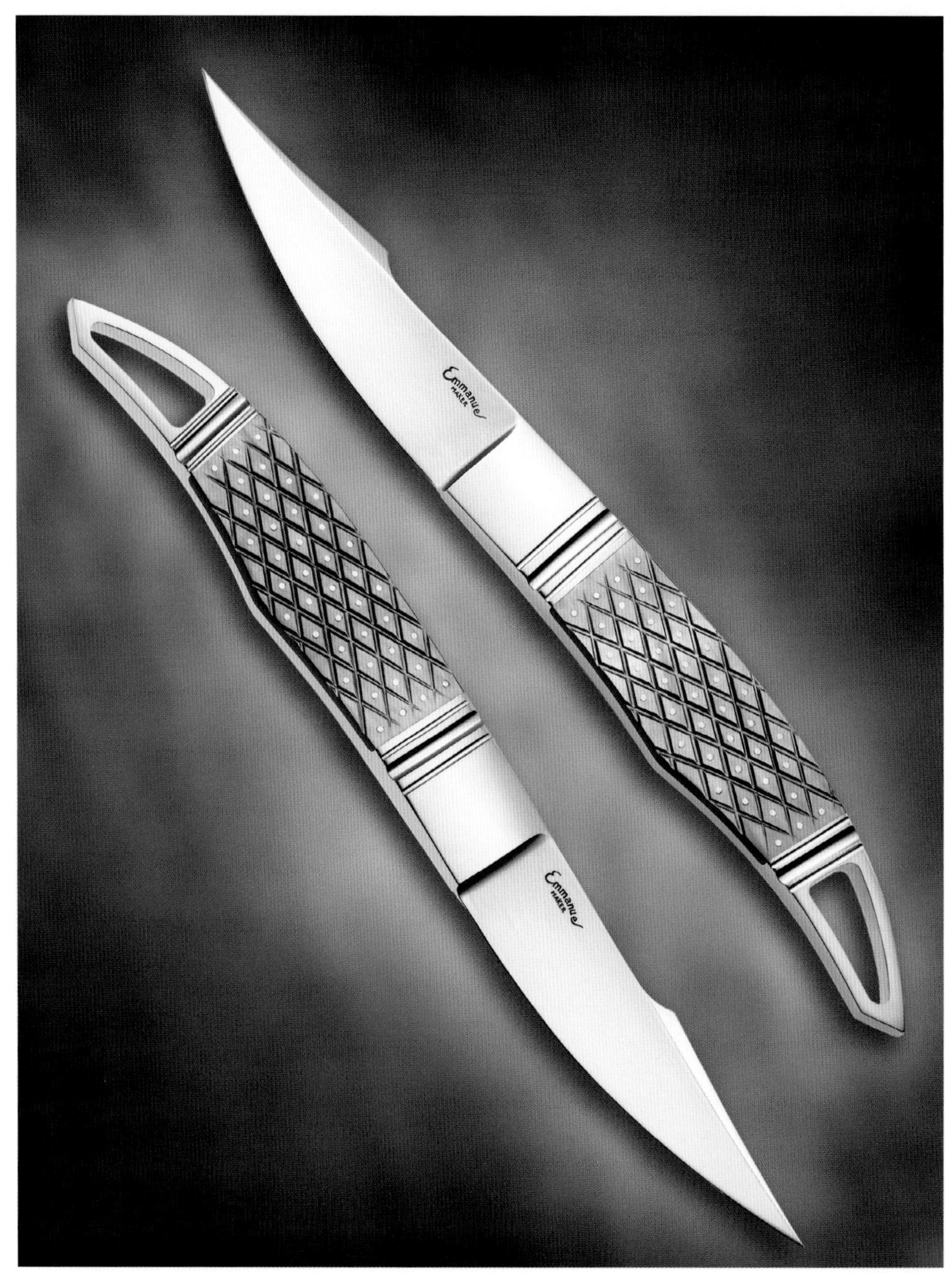

Emmanuel Esposito

Unicorn | 2007

OVERALL LENGTH, $7\frac{5}{16}$ INCHES (18.6 CM)

RWL-34 steel, black pearl, gold

PHOTO BY FRANCESCO PACHÍ

Owen Wood

Batwing Folding Knife | 2006

OVERALL LENGTH, 6 1/2 INCHES (16.5 CM)

Pinstripe and explosion composite Damascus steel, 303 stainless steel, titanium, mother-of-pearl; decorated, blued

PHOTO BY JIM COOPER OF SHARPBYCOOP.COM

Allen Elishewitz

Meteorite Scout | 2007

1 3/16 X 9 1/16 X 7/16 INCHES (3 X 23 X 1.2 CM)

Damascus steel, titanium, meteorite, opal, mother-of-pearl, black diamonds, stainless steel; drilled, machine cut

PHOTO BY VALERIE ELISHEWITZ

Robert Weinstock

Untitled | 2004

OVERALL LENGTH, 7 1/4 INCHES (18.5 CM)

Damascus steel, 14-karat gold; pierced, carved, chased

DAMASCUS STEEL BY ED SCHEMPP
PHOTO BY POINTSEVEN STUDIOS

Matthew Lerch

Rockford | 2008

OVERALL LENGTH, 6³⁄₈ INCHES (16.8 CM)

Double-stainless Damascus steel, Damascus steel, pen shell; inlaid, fluted

DOUBLE-STAINLESS DAMASCUS STEEL BY MIKE NORRIS
PHOTO BY JIM COOPER OF SHARPBYCOOP.COM

Juergen Steinau

Knife-Objekt 970923.1 | 1997

$8^1/_2$ X $1^1/_4$ X $^1/_2$ INCHES (21.6 X 3.2 X 1.3 CM)

440B stainless steel, pure nickel, black pearl

PHOTO BY POINTSEVEN STUDIOS

Salvatore Puddu

Watch-Pocket Folder | 2007

OVERALL LENGTH, 4 11/16 INCHES (12 CM)

Stainless steel; sculpted

PHOTO BY FRANCESCO PACHÍ

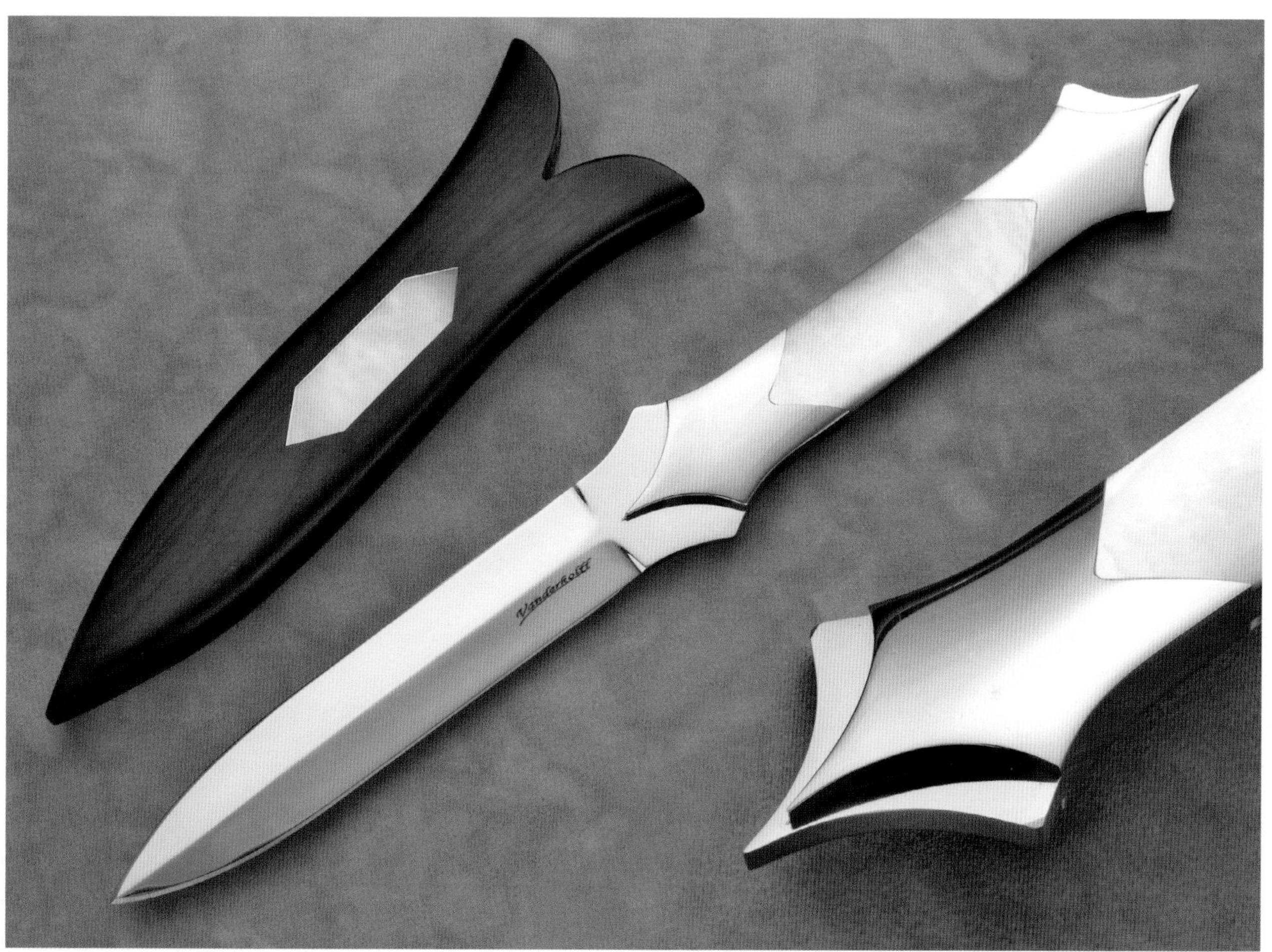

Steve Vanderkolff

Moon Dancer | 2005

OVERALL LENGTH, 10 1/2 INCHES (26.7 CM)

440C stainless steel, mother-of-pearl, African blackwood; mirror polished, inlaid

PHOTO BY JIM COOPER OF SHARPBYCOOP.COM

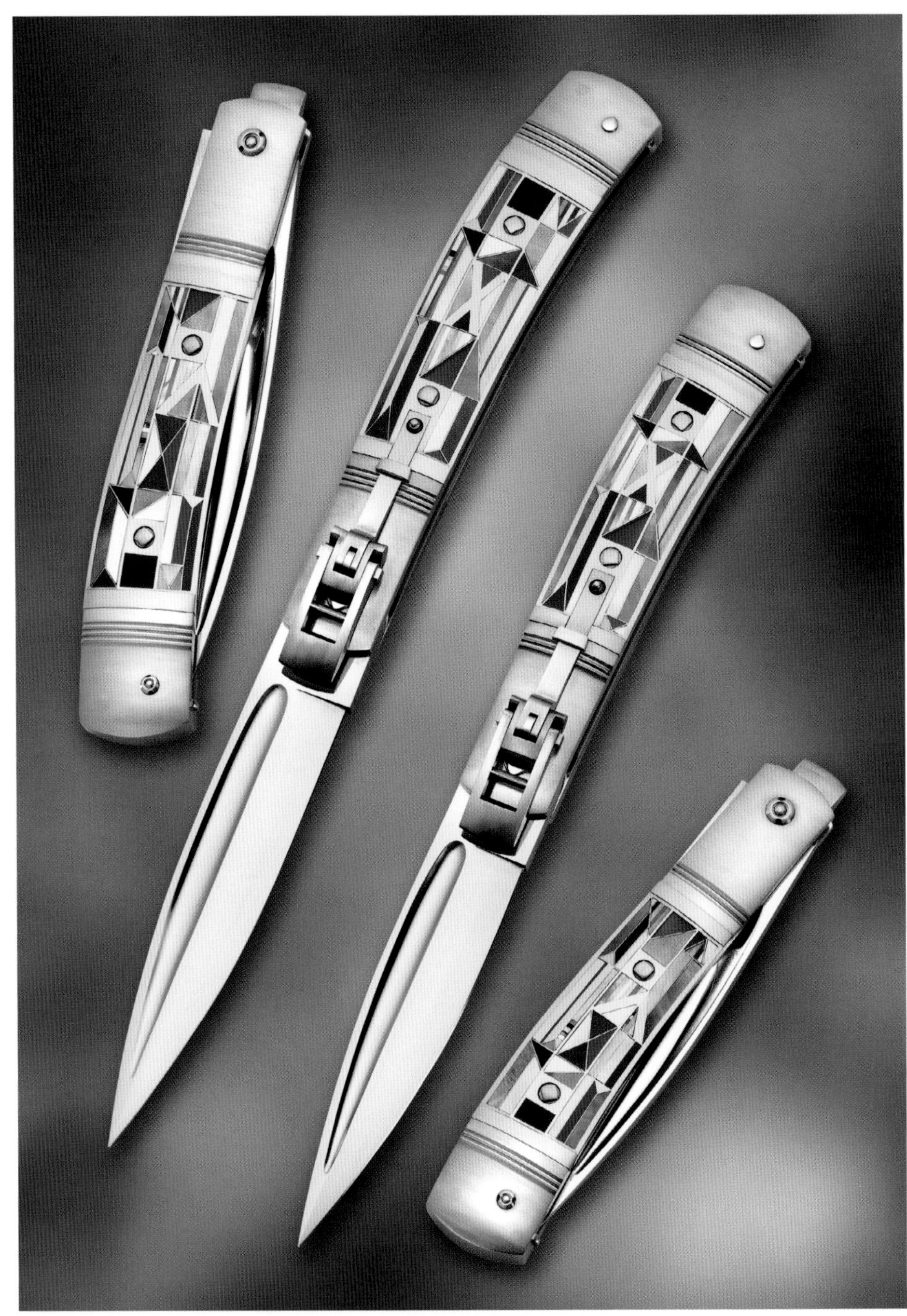

Jurgen Steinau

Art Deco Folders | 2001

OVERALL LENGTH, 8 5/8 INCHES (22 CM)

440B steel, nickel-copper alloy, pearl, stone, Bakelite, glass; inlaid

PHOTO BY FRANCESCO PACHÍ

Owen Wood

Art Nouveau Folding Knife | 2008

OVERALL LENGTH, 5 1/2 INCHES (14 CM)

Art deco Damascus steel, stainless Damascus steel, 303 stainless steel, 416 stainless steel, titanium; blued, engraved

ENGRAVED BY AMAYAK STEPANYAN
PHOTO BY JIM COOPER OF SHARPBYCOOP.COM

Dusty Moulton

The Talon | 2003

OVERALL LENGTH, 11 1/2 INCHES (29.2 CM)

CPM 154CM steel, 416 stainless steel, elephant ivory; engraved

PHOTO BY POINTSEVEN STUDIOS

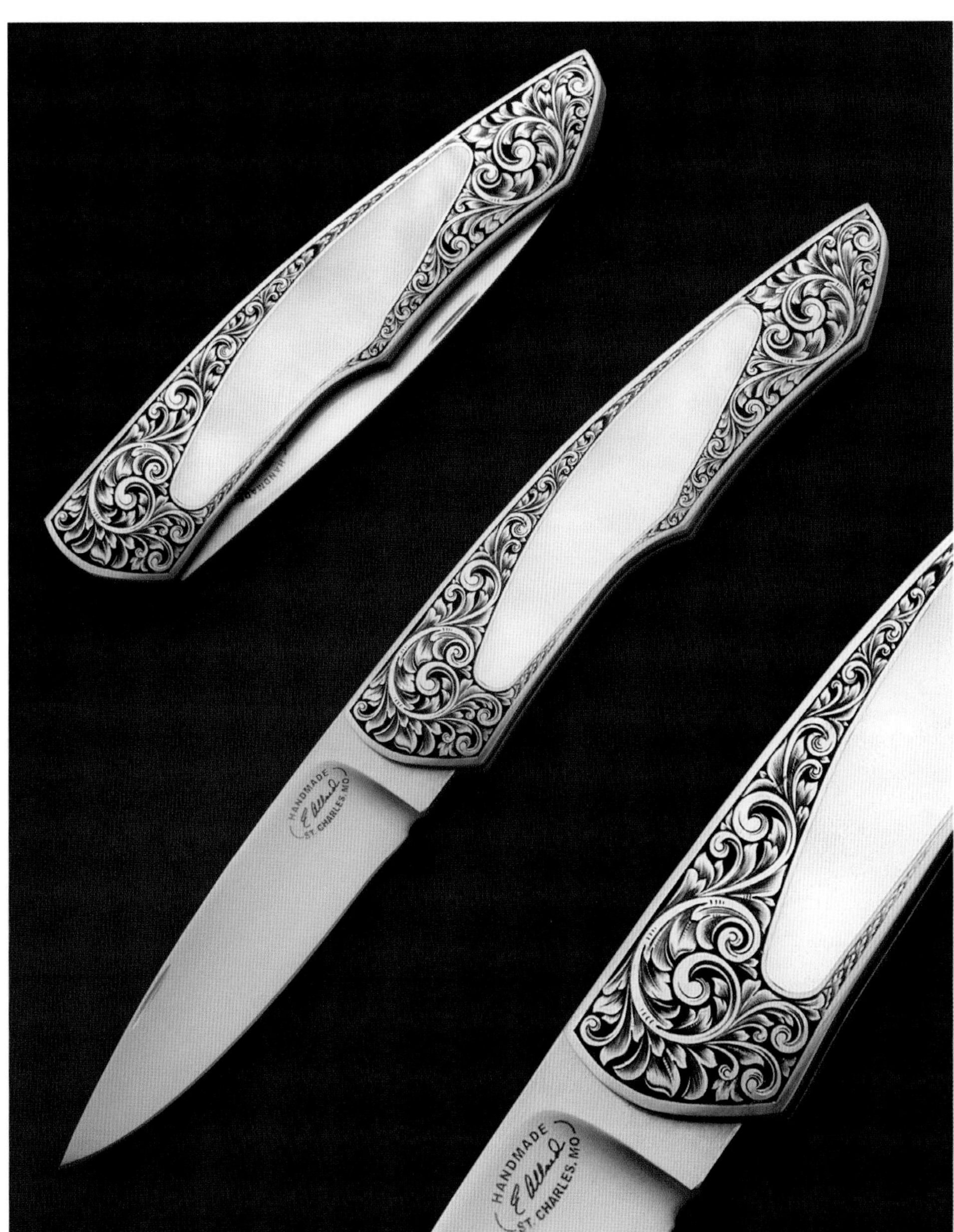

Elvan Allred

Allred/Carter #1 | 2007

OVERALL LENGTH, 6 INCHES (15.3 CM)

ATS-34 steel, 416 stainless steel, gold-lip mother-of-pearl; engraved, inlaid

DESIGNED BY SCOTT ALLRED
ENGRAVED BY DR. FRED CARTER
PHOTO BY DR. FRED CARTER

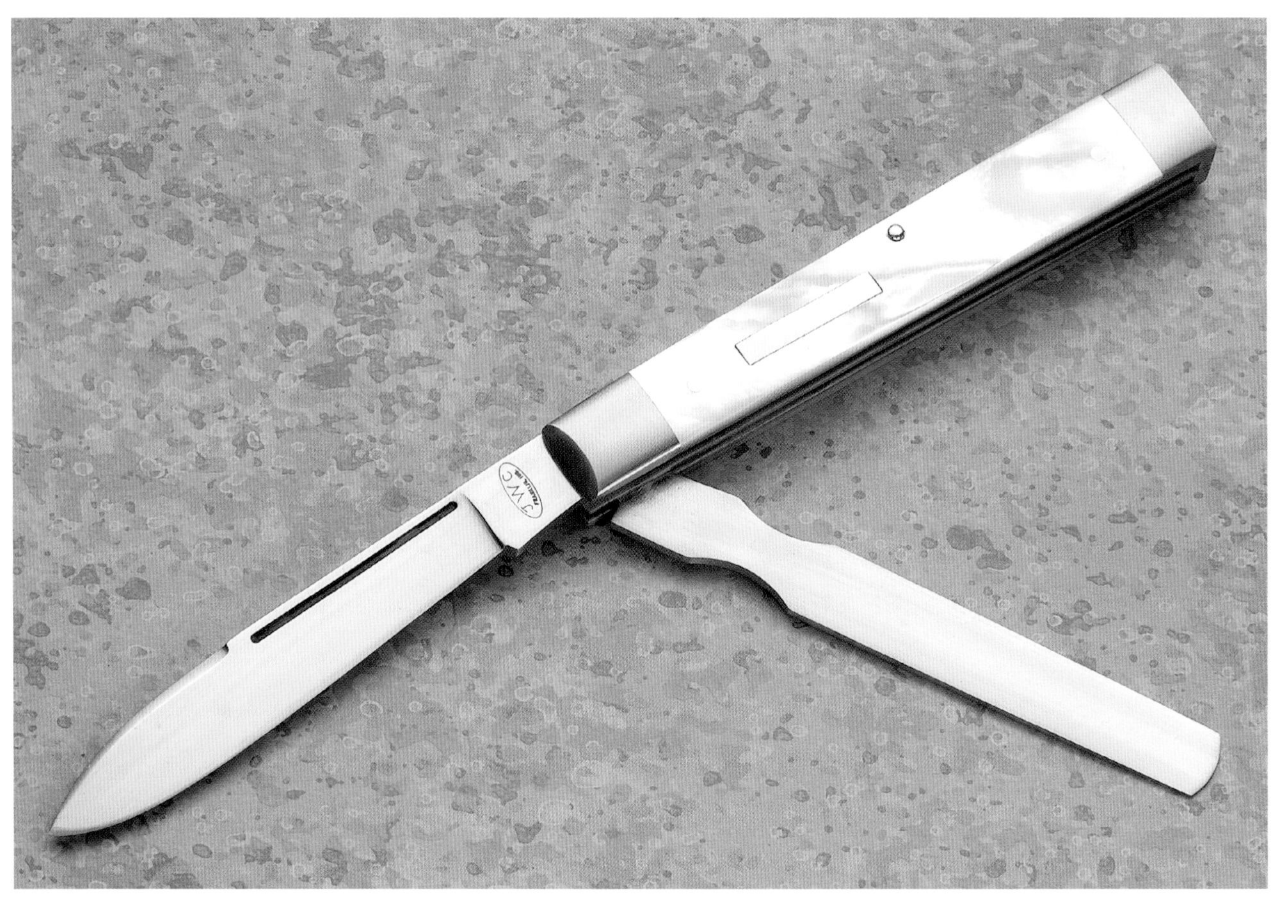

Jeff Claiborne

Doctor's Knife Blade and Spatula | 2007

$3^1/_8$ X $^1/_2$ X $^3/_8$ INCHES (7.9 X 1.3 X 1 CM)

52100 steel, 416 stainless steel, white pearl; forged, integral milled, ground

PHOTO BY TERRILL HOFFMAN

W.E. Ankrom

Frontlock | 2006

OVERALL LENGTH, 5¾ INCHES (14.6 CM)

Damascus steel, powder-metal mosaic Damascus steel, mother-of-pearl; stock removal

DAMASCUS STEEL BY MIKE NORRIS
POWDER-METAL MOSAIC DAMASCUS STEEL BY ROBERT EGGERLING
PHOTO BY JIM COOPER OF SHARPBYCOOP.COM

Scott Sawby

Kittiwake | 2005

OVERALL LENGTH, 6 13/16 INCHES (17.4 CM)

ATS-34 steel, 416 stainless steel, black-lip mother-of-pearl, Burmese jadeite; inlaid

PHOTO BY JIM COOPER OF SHARPBYCOOP.COM

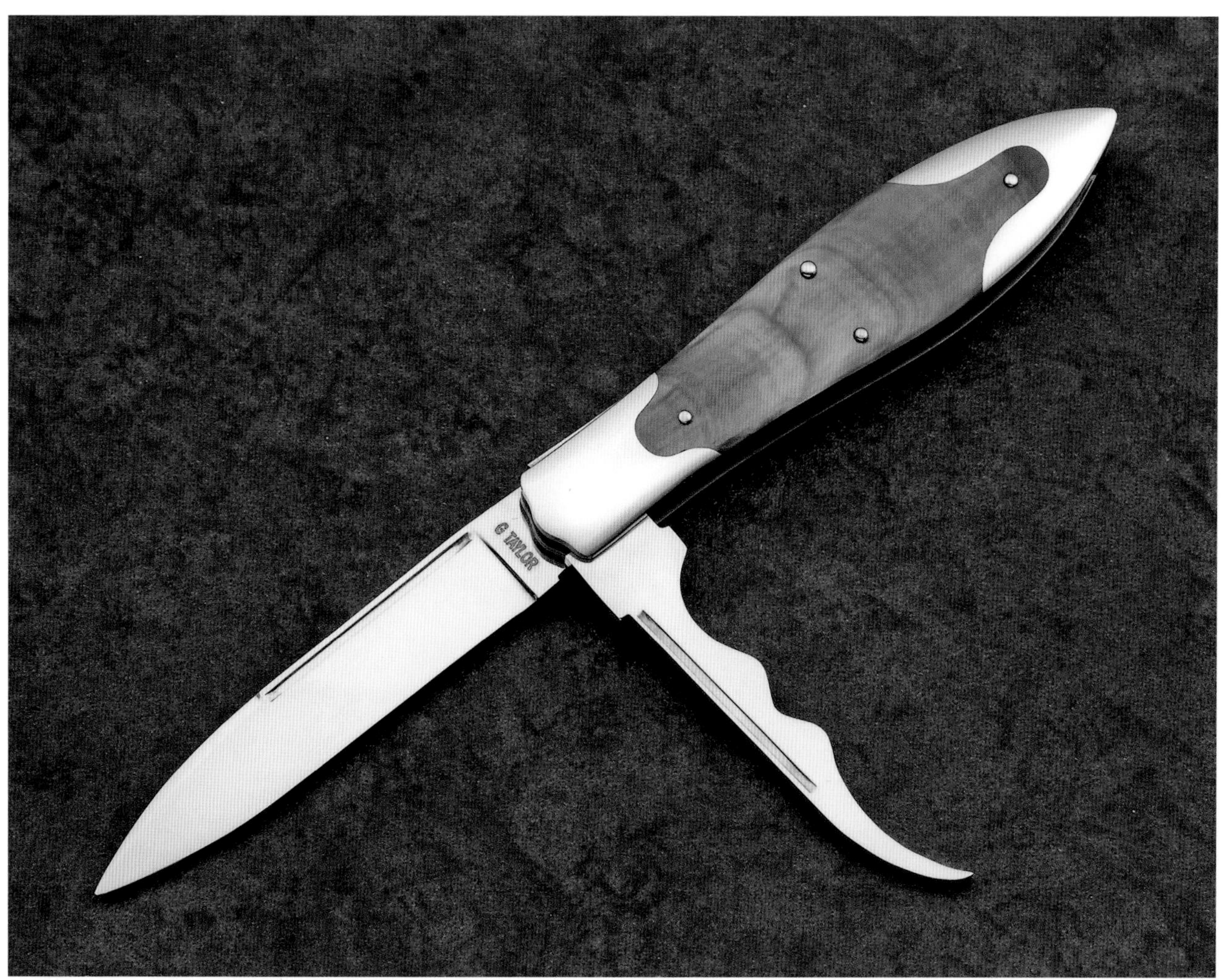

C. Gray Taylor

Folding Fruit Knife | 2006

OVERALL LENGTH, 5 7/8 INCHES (14.9 CM)

CPM 154 steel, 416 stainless steel, 14-karat gold, black-lip pearl

PHOTO BY JIM COOPER OF SHARPBYCOOP.COM

Charlie Bennica

Watch-Pocket Folder | 2005

5 1/16 INCHES (12.9 CM)

RWL-34 steel, 416 stainless steel, black-lip pearl, pearl; inlaid

PHOTO BY FRANCESCO PACHÍ

Lloyd Hale

Pipeline | 2005

440C stainless steel, abalone

PHOTO BY JIM COOPER OF SHARPBYCOOP.COM

W.E. Ankrom

Liner-Lock # 1-A1 | 2006

OVERALL LENGTH, 5 INCHES (12.7 CM)

Damascus steel, mother-of-pearl; stock removal, engraved

DAMASCUS STEEL BY MIKE NORRIS
ENGRAVED BY BRUCE SHAW
PHOTO BY JIM COOPER OF SHARPBYCOOP.COM

Rick Eaton

Art Deco Step Down Folding Dagger | 2007

OVERALL LENGTH, 8 3/16 INCHES (20.8 CM)

Stainless steel, black-lip pearl; engraved, inlaid

PHOTO BY POINTSEVEN STUDIOS

Reinhard Tschager

Mini Integral | 2001

OVERALL LENGTH, 4 3/16 INCHES (10.6 CM)

Gold, mother-of-pearl; engraved

ENGRAVED BY VALERIO PELI
PHOTO BY FRANCESCO PACHÍ

T.R. Overeynder

Model 25 Dagger | 2007

OVERALL LENGTH, 7 INCHES (17.8 CM)

Chevron and explosion Damascus steel, 416 stainless steel, nickel, black-lip pearl, 24-karat gold; engraved

BLADE STEEL BY OWEN WOOD
ENGRAVED BY JOE MASON
PHOTO BY JIM COOPER OF SHARPBYCOOP.COM

Contributing Artists

Allred, Elvan
St. Charles, Missouri
Page 365

Almquist, Carl Michael
Lövånger, Sweden
Page 180

Andrews II, Russ
Sugar Creek, Missouri
Page 47

Ankrom, W.E.
Cody, Wyoming
Pages 367, 372

Ansø, Jens
Sporup, Denmark
Page 163

Appleton, Ron
Bluff Dale, Texas
Page 285

Barnett, Van
St. Albans, West Virginia
Pages 13, 81, 123, 275

Bastian, Alistair
Mount Gambier, South Australia
Page 289

Bekic, Lilyana
San Diego, California
Page 232

Bennica, Charlie
Moulès-et-Baucels, France
Pages 226, 370

Bergh, Roger
Bygdeå, Sweden
Pages 101, 293, 327

Best, Ronald
Stokes, North Carolina
Pages 54, 263

Bojtoš, Arpád
Lučenec, Slovakia
Pages 22, 229

Bona, Marcin
Slupsk, Poland
Page 143

Booth, Philip
Ithaca, Michigan
Page 158

Bradshaw, Bailey
Diana, Texas
Page 303

Broadwell, David
Wichita Falls, Texas
Pages 45, 50, 58, 261

Brown, Rob
Emerald Hill, Port Elizabeth, South Africa
Pages 254, 257

Burkovski, Vladimir
Haifa, Israel
Pages 23, 297

Carrizzi, Phil
Grand Rapids, Michigan
Page 340

Carter, Fred
Wichita Falls, Texas
Pages 15, 75

Caston, Darriel K.
Sacramento, California
Page 204

Chard, Gordon R.
Iola, Kansas
Page 245

Chen, Yuan-Fan
Taichung, Taiwan
Pages 167, 187

Claiborne, Jeff
Franklin, Indiana
Pages 140, 366

Colter, Wade
Colstrip, Montana
Pages 98, 230, 241

Coogan, Robert
Silver Point, Tennessee
Pages 237, 343

Corbit, Gerald E.
Elizabethtown, Kentucky
Pages 82, 351

Cordova, Sherry
Sunnyvale, California
Page 267

Cornwell, Jeffrey
Anchorage, Alaska
Pages 88, 338, 341

Cowles, Don
Royal Oak, Michigan
Page 349

Crawford, Pat
West Memphis, Arkansas
Pages 65, 201, 218

Crawford, Wes
West Memphis, Arkansas
Pages 65, 201, 218

Cronin, Dave
Grand Rapids, Michigan
Page 340

Cucchiara, Matt
Fresno, California
Page 248

Dailey, George E.
Seekonk, Massachusetts
Pages 9, 25, 26, 77, 215, 278

Davidson, Edmund
Goshen, Virginia
Pages 35, 265, 333, 336

Davis, John
Selah, Washington
Page 157

Dean, Harvey
Rockdale, Texas
Pages 112, 330

Dellana
St. Albans, West Virginia
Pages 53, 80, 81

Deringer, Christoph
Cookshire, Canada
Page 144

Doussot, Laurent
Saint-Bruno, Quebec, Canada
Pages 153, 283

Dunkerley, Rick
Seeley Lake, Montana
Pages 126, 211, 286

Eaton, Rick
Broadview, Montana
Pages 36, 272, 373

Edwards, Mitch
Glasgow, Kentucky
Pages 298, 322

Elishewitz, Allen
New Braunfels, Texas
Pages 207, 296, 356

Embretsen, Kaj
Edsbyn, Sweden
Pages 66, 129, 195, 250, 319, 350

Erickson, Curt
North Ogden, Utah
Pages 8, 33, 321

Esposito, Emmanuel
Buttigliera Alta, Italy
Pages 142, 354

Evans, Vince
Cathlamet, Washington
Pages 85, 302, 346

Ferrero, Tom
Windsor, Connecticut
Pages 52, 91, 235

Fisk, Jerry L.
Nashville, Arkansas
Page 152

Flood, Frankie
Whitefish Bay, Wisconsin
Page 238

Fogarizzu, Antonio
Pattada, Italy
Pages 161, 316

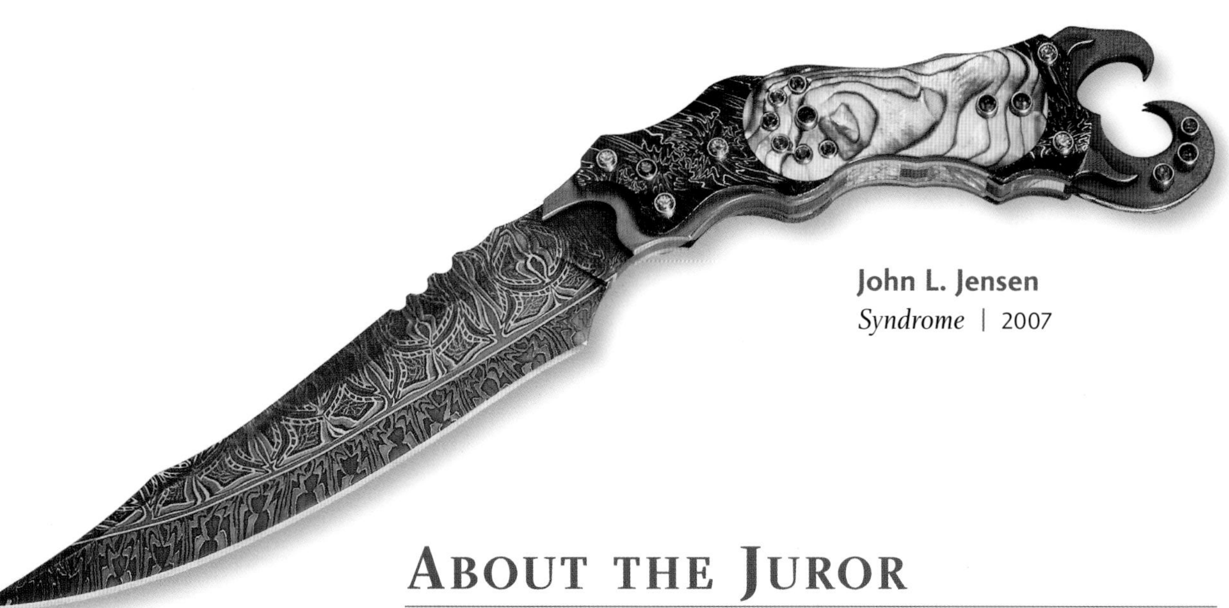

John L. Jensen
Syndrome | 2007

About the Juror

Born and raised in California, John L. Jensen has been promoting the knife as a creative art form for more than 15 years. A graduate of the Rhode Island School of Design, he holds a B.F.A. in jewelry and metalsmithing. Jensen has been featured in more than 60 publications, both national and international. In 2005 his work was included in *Metalsmith* magazine's annual juried competition, Exhibition in Print. Jensen has participated in numerous gallery shows, including Hammer and Hand: Contemporary American Metal at Calvin College in Grand Rapids, Michigan; The Influence of Rock and Roll at the Rock and Roll Hall of Fame and Museum in Cleveland, Ohio; and California Art Metal Now at the Blue Room Gallery in San Francisco, California.

Jensen is a frequent lecturer, and he conducts workshops regularly around the country. In 2007 he curated the first museum show of modern art knives at the National Ornamental Metals Museum in Memphis, Tennessee. He is a member of the American Bladesmith Society, the Society of North American Goldsmiths, and the Knife Maker's Guild. He lives in Los Angeles with his wife, Kristina.

ACKNOWLEDGMENTS

I am incredibly grateful for the expertise, enthusiasm, and generosity of our juror, John Jensen. His passion, determination, and good humor were unshakable as we worked to make the dream of *500 Knives* become real. John's clear and informed vision has shaped a truly unique collection of work.

Special thanks goes to Jim Cooper, whose exquisite photography graces so many of these pages. As a conduit to many of the featured artists, Jim was indispensible, and I am indebted for his advocacy and generosity. Jessica Marcotte created an outstanding image for the cover, and Kristina Keane-Jensen was supremely encouraging throughout.

Tom Ferrero
Moss Cutter | 2007

I deeply appreciate the support of the knifemakers from around the world who sent images to be considered for this series. I also wish to thank the galleries, schools, and organizations that promote contemporary knifemaking, teach and inspire others, and advocate our publications.

Publishing is an amazing collaborative adventure. It takes a talented team of professionals to manage the multitude of details that comprise these books. Julie Hale, Dawn Dillingham, Gavin Young, Rosemary Kast, and Janet Hurley provided indispensable editorial support. Chris Bryant, Shannon Yokeley, and Jeff Hamilton supplied first-rate assistance in the art department, and Kay Stafford gave us a truly gorgeous layout and design. Todd Kaderabek and Lance Wille kept us on schedule. I value your talent, effort, and friendship every day.

Marthe Le Van